P9-APW-609

Learning How Children Worship

The Cooperative Series

This book has been developed through the cooperative efforts of many denominations seeking to provide publications of sound educational values and practical usefulness through an interdenominational agency, the Cooperative Publication Association.

Grace W. McGavran

Learning
How
Children
Worship

Illustrated by James A. Scott

Published for
The Cooperative Publication Association
by
THE BETHANY PRESS
ST. LOUIS, MISSOURI

UNITY SCHOOL LIBRARY
DISCARD
Lee's Summit, Missouri 64063

© 1964 BY THE BETHANY PRESS

Library of Congress Catalog Card Number: 64-21304

All rights in this book are reserved. No part of the text may
be reproduced in any manner without permission in writing
from the publisher, except in the case of brief quotations included in a review of the book in a magazine or newspaper.

The Scripture quotations in this volume, unless otherwise in-
dicated, are from the Revised Standard Version of the Holy
Bible, copyrighted in 1946 and 1952 by the Division of
Christian Education, National Council of the Churches of
Christ in the U. S. A., and are used by permission.

MANUFACTURED IN THE UNITED STATES OF AMERICA

BV
1522
M171l

Contents

Contents

Introduction

This text is not planned to answer all your questions and wonderings about how children worship, but to help you to think along certain lines and find many of your own answers to your own specific problems.

The procedures are planned to help you consider and evaluate where you are, the materials you use, the physical arrangements in which you work, and the persons who can be helpful to you. You will be helped to look at the children, their parents, other adults, and to try to think into their patterns and experiences of worship.

You will hear from others in the study group and will read in this text what is going on that might interest you, and will guide you in what to do and what to avoid.

The procedures should help you to experiment and analyze what you are planning; what is happening.

As you, alone, with your own church group, or with a group from many churches, read and work with this book, you will find enrichment and growth in worship made possible not only for the children, but for you yourself.

Throughout the text there are sections planned to help you to analyze, think, plan, sense, and be ready to make the most of opportunities for worship. These are indicated by lines set in smaller type. They are not pronouncements of principles but exercises to be done by each individual using this book. If you can use these sections as you come to them—not at the end of a chapter or a session in a leadership school—they probably will be more meaningful to you. As you do this, you yourself will be growing in ability to respond to God in worship.

presence.

1.   *The Heart of Worship*

What Is Worship?

Someone has said, "Worship is becoming conscious
of the ever-present presence of God." Certainly, nothing short of this is worship, although worship can and
often does go far beyond it.

"Becoming conscious of the ever-present presence of
God!" For most persons this is the heart of worship.
" 'Be still, and know that I am God!' " the psalmist
said. Only as a person, either adult or child, becomes
quiet and aware is he able to worship.

The following relates an experience which probably
has happened to everyone in one way or another. A
woman is very busy weeding her flower garden. It is
close to sunset and she works furiously. All about her
the sky flames into glory, but she does not see it. Then
she looks up! In that moment, as she stands in delight
and wonder, the garden, its roses, and its weeds drop
from her consciousness, and all that she sees and feels
is the glorious light transfiguring all it touches.

The sky was ablaze with color long before she noticed it. Even so, God's presence is around, about, and

within every person; but many are too occupied with the affairs of daily life to be much, if at all, aware of his presence.

Yet, as that woman suddenly became so aware of the beauty of the sky that all else faded from her consciousness, so each one at times becomes aware to the depths of his being of the presence of God. God was there all the time, but he was unnoticed. As minds turn to him, everything else fades into insignificance.

The psalmist said, " 'Be still.' " That is, lay aside all other thoughts and pursuits, and become quiet in body and mind and spirit.

The same writer added, " 'And know that I am God!' " or turn attention without reserve to God's presence.

Those who have worshiped in a silent meeting of the Friends, know how the silence deepens until the overwhelming consciousness of God's presence opens the heart to communion with him. However, such communion is not in the pattern of most worshiping groups, and this depth is found only in fleeting moments in most forms of group worship.

• Think back to a time when you became conscious of the presence of God in an especially deep way. Think of a moment in corporate worship with juniors, at home with the family, or in a Sunday church school class or department, when all in the group were united in a special awareness of God's presence. As you approach your own personal time of devotion, try disciplining yourself to take time to be aware of God's presence; not rushing at him with words, but being quiet and knowing that he is Lord. This is not an easy discipline. For those not practicing it, attention wanders in a very few seconds. Is one then to be content to be aware of

God only when speaking to him? Or is it worth the disciplining of self to be wordless in his presence that he may speak?

After Awareness, Acts of Worship

It has already been said that the heart of worship is the becoming aware of the presence of God. Such awareness in most groups and for many individuals is preliminary to response to God.

Worship may be viewed in two ways. One is the response to God's seeking awareness. This may be defined in terms of adoring, wondering, praising, thanksgiving, making petition, expressing contrition, and committing oneself to do God's will. The other may be considered as a means of worship such as prayer, singing, and the giving of an offering.

For example, a group of kindergarten children, after talking about the lovely things they have seen in springtime and singing "In My Little Garden Bed," are guided into conversation about God's plans for growing things. In this way the boys and girls gain an awareness of God's presence in his springtime world, whereas, before the conversation, there may have been only the enjoyment of springtime. Then comes the moment when the children are ready to respond not just with wonder and delight in the world, but with wonder and delight in God's wisdom and love. Now they can eagerly thank God for all that surrounds them and for his plans for the world. For response to become worship, it must be response to God, not just response to beauty, to nature, or to anything besides God himself.

Think of a group of juniors at camp on a mountainside. It is evening, the campfire is lit and everyone is

11

sitting around it. A hymn has been sung and with it has come a feeling of nearness to God. A leader tells a story or presents an idea that guides the thoughts of the juniors to their responsibility in their situation. A prayer follows in which recognition is made of the responsibility of children of God, and the hearts of the juniors give assent by determining to obey God's will for their behavior. As they pray, they are responding to God's will and dedicating their lives to him.

If this is not so, and if the juniors are just responding to the leader's presentation of "what we ought to do," it is not worship. Only as an act of dedication or as an offering of themselves to God is it worship.

Awareness of the presence of God is the heart of worship. Response to God is the heart of acts of worship.

It is difficult to be responsible for leading others into possibilities for worship. This means knowing how to lead, what approaches to make, what to say or do or have the group say or do; to be aware of what worship is and what it isn't, and to look critically at what is going on. It is difficult because it is not easy to worship while thinking, "Is this making worship possible for these first-graders?" or, "What is happening in the minds of the sixth-grade children that is keeping this hymn from leading them into an awareness of God's presence?" It is not easy for a leader to worship when he is concerned about Johnny who is in a hilarious mood and is preventing the whole group from experiencing any sense of worship.

Those who would help make worship meaningful for children must experience worship. From time to time, evaluate what is happening in your group. For example, you may need to quiet Johnny, then, with serenity, resume your own worship. It is essential, too, that you do not become so deeply involved in your personal worship within the group that you are oblivious to that for which you have assumed the responsibility: to help the children open their hearts to God by providing the place, the time, the words, and the atmosphere which will aid them to do so.

● Recall a moment when the children with whom you work felt and expressed real thankfulness to God. Recall a moment of loving praise. Recall a moment of determination to do right. Recall a time when you felt in them a real desire for God's help in some undertaking or problem. Go over in your mind the last worship time you had with children, or in an adult group if you have not worshiped recently with children, and consider whether there was any act intended to be worship which was not. Why was it not? On what was the attention centered rather than on God? What distraction outside or within the persons prevented worship? In what act did you sense real worship? What caused it? Was there any point at which you could have helped the moment to become one of real worship? What were you doing, physically and mentally, during each aspect of worship?

Some Definitions

Think of the various aspects of worship—the ways in which we respond to God. Try to define some of them. You will probably find yourself formulating other definitions as you think about worship with children. You may enlarge at some points the ones given here; at other points you may make your definitions more narrow. What you find here is just a suggestion to start you thinking along these lines.

1. *Call to Worship.* A call to worship causes attention to turn from self and the surroundings, or from extraneous thoughts, to God. For kindergarten children, this may be a simple question: "Would you like to say 'thank you' to God for brothers and sisters?" It may be a scripture verse which definitely says, "Come now and worship." It may be the tune of a worship hymn which will carry its message through its remembered words. It may be a place so imbued with the custom of worship that just entering it calls the heart to readiness for response to God. Usually, a call to worship is from leader to group. Sometimes it is the entire group using scripture or a hymn calling each other to worship:

> O come and let us worship!
> O come and let us worship!
> O come and let us worship, God our Lord!

● How do you help your group to turn their thoughts from self, extraneous ideas, and surroundings to God? In family worship? At the campfire? Before formal worship? At other times? Think about the atmosphere of the places of worship, or the moment of worship, the attitude of adults who are present, the words or music or expression which you use. Think of some way which you have not used but will try.

2. *Affirmation of Desire to Worship.* Whatever gives the worshiper the opportunity to feel or state that he is glad or happy to come to worship is such an affirmation. The psalm verse,

I was glad when they said to me,
"Let us go to the house of the Lord!"

is another. The hymn by William Bullock, "We love the place, O God, wherein thine honor dwells," is still another. The leader's statement, "How happy we are that we can come together today for study and worship," fulfills this function. It may even be possible that nothing is said or sung, but the happy faces and attitudes of those who have gathered express it.

- Are the children aware of the times of worship and what it should be for them—a conscious effort to enter into the presence of God with heart and spirit ready to respond to God's loving outreach to them? Or, are the children in your group unaware of what worship really is? Are other teachers, parents, and workers aware? Is your joy in the privilege of communion with God so apparent that even a young child will want to find what you are finding? Is there ringing delight and sincerity in the affirmations you use? Do you sometimes use affirmations; sometimes use calls to worship? Do you sometimes let the place speak, or let adult attitudes prepare for worship? If you have not been using affirmation fruitfully, consider what will make its use effective. This study is to help you, in your family or wherever you are with children, to grow in helping them open their hearts to God. Only you can put its suggestions to trial in your own situation.

3. *Hymns of Praise and Adoration.* There are two classes of such hymns: those addressed to God; those which are affirmations about God. With hymns of these two types, there may be included the spoken word such as is found in a psalm, a poem, or rich prose passages.

15

"Praise to the Lord, the Almighty," is of the second type. So is "Sing Praises, Sing Praises to God." Psalm 100, with its fourth verse a call to worship, is this type.

"Joyful, Joyful, We Adore Thee," is of the first type. So is "Come, Thou Almighty King." The response, "For every lovely thing, We give thanks to thee, O Lord," is another. The first stanza of "Gladly Lift We Hearts and Voices," is direct praise. Psalm 138 speaks directly to God.

Notice that the above list includes hymns which speak directly to God in thanksgiving for material things. This kind of hymn does have its place but, too often, is centered on the things, not on God! For instance, one song for primary children begins, frankly, "Dear God, we thank you for ourselves," and goes on putting the stress on self. Even its second stanza brings the thoughts back to self. This prayer hymn and others like it have their place in petition, but they are not praise of God, which is now being considered.

- In an adult or a junior hymnal, find hymns of praise to God, or those that proclaim his praise to others. Be sure that God is the center of such hymns, rather than what he has done for men. Find any such hymns in primary or kindergarten music. "Sing Praises, Sing Praises to God" proclaims God's praise. Other hymns children sing are addressed directly to God to say, "We praise you God!" or "We love you God!" Such expressions of love and devotion to God are made just because he is God. Look in the sentences set to music in the back of many children's hymnals. Often these are lovely words addressed directly to God. Whatever age group you are working with, select two sentences or hymns that you think would help your children to open their hearts through direct speech to praise God. Be sure they are not merely thanksgiving to God for what he has given!

4. *Thankfulness to God.* How richly the soul can have communion with God through expressions of thankfulness! It is much easier to concentrate upon the goodness, greatness, and nature of God himself in which praise is given just because God is God and not because of material benefit gained. But thankfulness is an important facet of one's relationship to God. That habit of mind which turns a loving glance of thanks toward God, as well as that which utters thanksgiving in the spoken word or a hymn, is one to cultivate in children if they are to grow in being aware of God's presence.

The pastor who prayed, thanking God for a new church building, did so knowing, as did all his congregation, young and old, that only with God's help had that group of people overcome the difficulties in the way of securing the place of worship that now was being dedicated. There was true thanksgiving, and every child felt around him the assent of the older people to the idea that it was God and not they who was responsible for the building in which they were assembled for the first time. The heart of worship may include bowing low in real thankfulness and in intelligent understanding of the fact that God has made possible certain things.

A problem to be faced is the tendency to accept as from God all that is good and reject all that is bad as having anything at all to do with his will. Give thanks for discipline? Give thanks for hardship? Give thanks for suffering? Even a child can begin to understand that God would not have put him in a world where such things exist if these had not some function in growth. Worship involves trust in God's wisdom. It also involves accepting the fact that the full extent of God's will cannot be known. In other words, a person cannot know whether something happens because it is God's will or is contrary to his will, but it is permitted for reasons which cannot be seen. Adults can help themselves and their children to realize that as they face difficulty and hardship they may come to thank God for what seemed at the time unendurable; that his merciful guidance and strength can be counted on in the most sorrowful times. Worship turns one toward God, knowing that he is with the individual through it. It does not ignore God nor fail to thank him for his concern just because circumstances are as they are.

- How would you guide your children to pray in thanksgiving to God when thinking of the beauties of spring, if there is a blind child in the class? What other senses can help the blind child to rejoice in springtime? Can one child's blindness help the others to find new rejoicing and thankfulness through the usually ignored senses of feeling, scent, and taste? Write a prayer of thankfulness that could be used by a family whose father is failing to provide at all for his family but, instead, is wasting money in foolish ways. Mention situations in which the prayer of thankfulness should be modified because of temporary conditions which could cause rejection of the prayer by some child in the group. Will the modification help that child to lay hold upon the goodness of God, and increase his trust in God's love and concern? In the weeks ahead, note if the children really are rejoicing in God's good gifts and are having real joy in expressing their thanks whether spoken or sung.

5. *Finding Out What God's Will Is.* It has been said previously that God is reaching out to men, and that worship is their awareness of and response to him. In

this sense, seeking to know the will of God can be worship. It is very difficult to tell the difference between opening the heart to God for guidance and trying in one's own power to decide what to do. Yet, as teachers, you must present to children what it is hoped God can use to reveal his will to them.

At a monthly meeting of the Friends a concern that was discussed was whether or not it was right to bring a Bible to worship. To anyone not accustomed to the Friends' procedures, the very question was startling. There was a great deal of silence and seeking of guidance from God before there was found what seemed to all to be God's will. The conclusion was that if a person searches in the Bible to find what he thought the rest should hear and brought his Bible to meeting and read aloud that passage, he had better leave the Bible at home. But if he brought the Bible to meeting, ready to feel the stirring of God in his heart to read a passage in the meeting, it was well to have the Bible there that he might follow God's leading.

To those who most carefully prepare scripture reading, talks, and stories beforehand, does this suggest that God can best speak to human need through scripture and prayer if his guidance is sought as the material is chosen?

Leadership in worship is a sacred task. The person who comes before any group, flipping the pages of a hymnbook or the Bible, saying, "I've not prepared much but I'm sure we'll have a wonderful time of worship," is not likely to fulfill his function. He needs to be thoroughly prepared if he is to guide the group into the attitude and through experiences which will help them to feel God's presence, and to respond to God in praise, petition, determination, dedication, or understanding.

19

God can speak to his children through what is chosen and done. Only he can guide their leaders in choosing wisely what can serve his great purposes.

● If you are with children of kindergarten age, you need to know by heart Bible stories, songs, poems, Bible verses, and other material so that you can use them freely without reference to a book. What guides your choice of what to learn? Have you sat quietly before God, seeking his guidance as to what will best nurture his children so that they may sense his presence and respond to him in happy, loving ways? Have you taken time to learn what God has guided you to know will be useful from time to time, or have you withdrawn into "I don't have time to learn that. I guess this old one will do." Perhaps a first question is, "Do you really practice seeking the guidance of God?" This is a very personal question for each one to think about; but what might be helpful to consider is whether or not you do believe that God can give this help, and whether some can speak of having been so guided so that others will be encouraged to seek such help.

Jesus revealed God's will through unforgettable stories and teachings. Do you know where to find, without hesitation, the verses, stories, and passages in the Bible which will, under God, be helpful to primary and junior children? Have you learned to tell stories through which God can speak to a child of the age you are leading? Are you richly armed for your task, or are your biblical and other armaments meager? As you yourself read the Bible, do you ask, "Is this something to be used with children?" Remember that much prayerful thought has been given to selecting scripture and other materials in the various curriculum guides. You will find your quarterlies, teacher's and pupil's materials, rich in resources for instant recall. There may be occasions when these will be even more meaningful than in the one session where their use is suggested.

6. *Something to Think About.* It is curious how thinking along one line may shed light in quite a different direction. This chapter is concerned with the heart of worship. The use of scripture and other materials through which God may speak to persons in the service of worship has been discussed. But suppose that the scripture has not been used in the service of worship? Suppose that it has been used in a class period? Suppose that there has been discussion following the reading?

A teacher had a class of restless junior-age boys and girls. Without time for preparation, she was substituting for a teacher who had been unable to come at the last minute. The children didn't know her, she didn't know the children. Not a very desirable situation! However, she used some procedures she had found useful in other such situations and gained the attention and interest of the children. She found out something of their abilities. Then she told the story from the Bible that a hasty glance at the materials had shown to be the basic material from the scriptures for that day. The children became very quiet. Then they talked about Nicodemus and what they thought he must have done after Jesus talked with him. Somehow they began to understand that a person can begin again with God's help, as if he were a newborn baby, and can live a totally different kind of life. The message of the story came to them just as surely as if it had been used in a worship service. Here, right now, was the time of understanding. Here was the moment for thanksgiving to God for his love and mercy and his fresh beginnings for those who turn to him. Here was the heart of worship.

The basis for worship is a heart made ready for it, rather than a time set aside for it. One of the most difficult things for teachers and parents of children to see is that while there is need to set aside a regular time and prepare for it, spontaneous worship may mean more than all the rest put together.

Many persons are reticent about that for which they care most deeply. They are ashamed to show any emotion. They are ashamed to speak about God among their friends in casual conversation, but they are ready enough to talk about religion when religion is the subject. Often persons do not talk about God in their homes at all, except at such times as are set apart to do so. This habit of thought prevents adults at home, as teachers and as leaders, from flooding life with the light of acknowledgment of God's presence.

If children are to be helped to be aware of the presence of God, this reluctance must be overcome. Hearts and minds must be disciplined to a more constant turning of thoughts to God. There must be watchful attention for times when it is as natural to say, "I just can't imagine how God could plan such an intricate thing as this flower!" as to exclaim, "O look, the sun is shining!"

This is not to say that children can be pushed into an awareness of God's presence. Your own radiant awareness of God can lead their thoughts toward him, as he seeks them. You must sense that they are ready for it before you do very much about it. The children themselves will come to volunteer such comments, if your guidance is skillful. Unless you are guiding them into the habit of turning to God, you are in danger of getting the reaction, "She's forever dragging God into everything!" as one junior put it.

Some juniors were ending a party with a hilarious mood that would have sent them all out laughing and shouting. The teacher in charge blew a whistle. With great difficulty the giggling children grew quiet enough to hear. "We'll end our party by thanking God for our good time," she said sternly, and prayed.

"Why did she have to go and ruin the end of the party," growled Anthony, going out with a scowl on his face. No one recaptured the gay hilarity of the occasion.

Boys and girls accustomed to turning to God would have, between laughs, individually thought, "Haven't we had a wonderful time, God?" seeing God's laughter and smiles right with them.

Children can be guided to be aware of God in love and gratitude and thanksgiving throughout the hours of their days, and to respond to his will in determination to carry it out in their lives.

• Think of the group you lead, teach, or guide in your home. How often in this past week or in your last session did the moment arise when you could help the children to worship? In class, you can lead deliberately to this moment, although you cannot force its achievement. Think back. Were there times when you could have lifted your eyes from the information you were sharing or the attitudes you were cultivating and have seen God's glory about you, and lifted the children's minds and hearts with yours to a quick awareness of God in your midst? This is not easy to do. But is it not the heart of all teaching, all services of worship, all life, to respond to God himself?

During this next week, take time to let God speak to you. Take time to think about him—meditate upon him—as the psalms say. Take time to consider the world, the things, and the people about you as belonging to God. Take time to lift your eyes from the tasks of the moment and let the glory of his presence crowd all else from your mind and soul.

2. What Helps Children to Want to Worship?

The title of this chapter is intentionally worded as it is. Sometimes it is easy to forget that children cannot be made to worship. They cannot even be given an experience of worship. All that can be done is to provide the atmosphere, the opportunity, and the means through which they may worship if they have a desire to do so.

It is hard to say which is the most important preparation to make. The following suggestions are not presented in any order of importance. Each person needs to determine for himself which seems to be most important. Even then there will be exceptions. For instance, although quiet is ordinarily conducive to worship, there may be a time when the frantic confusion of untoward circumstances will impell the child to turn to God in a cry for help or comfort. What is suggested here, then, is the ordinary objective of preparation for leading children into what may open doors of worship.

Worshiping Adults

A certain church became for many of its members a place of unusual opportunities for worship made possible by several factors. One of these was the way in which the choir came in, faces radiant, steps firm, voices joyful, attitude proclaiming, "We are coming into the presence of God, and our attention is centered on him!" The minister, too, as he entered and took his place, somehow conveyed that this for him was a sacred hour. In that assumption of worship by its leadership, the people were drawn into a sense of being in the presence of God.

You may say, "But this was an adult service." Very true. But contrast this scene.

A Primary Department superintendent stood before the group of children calling out directions for them to take their places. She darted from her place at the front of the room to separate two small boys. The first-grade teacher was busy getting pictures from the file. The second-grade teacher was chatting with the third-grade teacher in the back row. The pianist was hunting through the music for something she wanted. Finally, she began to play, but the other adults continued their preoccupations. A visiting parent came in and joined those in conversation in the rear seats. There seemed to be no consciousness, during the worship time, that those present were mentally "coming into the presence of God." While the children possibly did experience some moments of worship, it was not because of adult concentration upon worship. Adults should be disciplined persons. They can prepare themselves for worship, and it is their responsibility to do so. Just as the choir and minister, by conscious concentration upon entering the presence of God, helped the congregation to feel the moment as one of worship, so the adults in any children's group either aid the boys and girls to worship, or hinder and keep them from it. The one in leadership has, of course, a dual role: responsibility for what happens and as a worshiper. But every adult in the room has the responsibility for entering into worship wholeheartedly. Worshiping adults help children to want to worship and to become able to do so.

● Now, and also at a later time, evaluate ten groups entering upon a period of worship. If adult groups, what attitude on the part of which adults is centering the thoughts of all on worship? If children's groups, what is each adult doing that will help or hinder the children from feeling, "We are coming into a special and wonderful time of being close to God!" What is your own custom during the moments preceding the opening of formal worship? Try to improve your own attitude and performance as one who makes it possible for others to enter into the holiness of worship. This course will not mean much to you unless you deliberately evaluate your own as well as the attitudes and actions of other adults, and reach toward a deeper ability to worship and to help others worship.

In a certain home, the moment comes for offering the prayer of thanks for food. The father pauses, and then, somehow, what is so often a swift repetition of "grace before meals" becomes a moment when God's presence is felt in that room, with humble adoration and thanks being offered. It is a worship experience for every guest in that home, a moment vibrant with communion.

There are many moments of informal worship with children; many times when just a few words of prayer or praise are uttered. But it depends largely on the adult whether or not such a vivid sense of communion with God is felt that the children themselves feel his presence and enter into the joy of real prayer. A worshiping adult conveys the reality of worship as no mere instruction about worship or mere "leading in worship" can do.

● When you are with a group of children, check to see whether you yourself are really worshiping or merely leading the children to worship. This may be as an adult with one or two children at home, at church school, at camp, before meals, or at any other place or time when you pray with or in behalf of boys and girls. Discipline yourself to the practice of real prayer so that, increasingly, you are able to convey a rich sense of your own consciousness of God's presence as you pray.

Orderliness and Beauty

Mrs. Jones slaves for a week to get ready for her club meeting. Everything must be spotless. But her Junior Department room, where the juniors are to come in a special way into communion with God, is a mess. This most important encounter with him in whom they live and move and have their being is to take place in the midst of disorder and unloveliness. There is nothing to say, "Here is our church home, made spotless and beautiful for the moments of each week when we gather together to praise and adore our God, to confess our shortcomings and seek help, to acknowledge our corporate relationship to him."

Stark simplicity may be orderly. Physical arrangements may bespeak attention paid to the holiness of the place where God and man are joined in worship.

There may be conscious effort to bring the orderliness into such relationships that there is beauty. One Junior Department had to carry chairs from where the class met to where the group's sharing period took place. This included worship. The space was large; but experimentation determined the best placement of the chairs to create the feeling of being a worshiping body rather than a sprawling assembly. A focal point was created to give beauty and balance of arrangement. This provided a physical readiness for worship.

- For moments of corporate worship, do your children all face toward whatever you have planned for them to center their attention? Are all things always in order? Are physical arrangements such that they are satisfying? Is there plenty of space for individual comfort? Are all unnecessary objects removed which would distract the worshiping group? As you look at the corner, room, or place of worship before a teacher or child is present, does it say, "Come and let us worship"? If not, what changes should be made? Who should make them? What can you, an individual, do to take care of bringing orderliness and beauty into the only place of worship that some children in your group will ever know?

Music

One of the best aids to worship is music. Quiet, meditative music, or the tune to a hymn customarily used that is worshipful, will bring the thoughts of children and adults from what has occupied them to the time when they are to "be still" and join in worship.

Music must be well chosen for such a purpose. The tune of "Friends! Friends! Friends!" for instance, does not call one to quietness and worship. Nor does "I Would Be True." Hymns or songs with familiar words but words not concerned with the approach to God, distract the thought and are not a wise choice for preparing the children and helping them feel God's seeking presence. This music is suitable in its place, which is not to prepare for worship. Rather, choose the hymn tune used with "Joyful, Joyful, We Adore Thee," or "For the Beauty of the Earth." Possibly better than hymn tunes are wordless selections of the meditative type, chosen from simple collections of appropriate music.

• Does the "quiet" music used with your group call attention to the fact that all are now withdrawing themselves from what has been occupying them and are centering their thoughts on God? If hymn tunes are being used, are they played meditatively? Are the words, which the children may recall when hearing the music, suitable for this moment? Are the musical selections ones which will say to children and adults alike, "O come, and and let us worship?" Find others that you think would well serve such a purpose.

Wordless guidance through music is not its only function in worship. Music and words of hymns that are chosen can increase the desire for worship.

A church school department's time of worship was opened with "Onward Christian Soldiers." It was sung listlessly, since there was nothing at the moment to carry forward with enthusiasm. It did not draw the thoughts to God, for it spoke as one person to others.

It was a song of encouragement, not a hymn to God. Another time of worship was opened with the hymn "With Happy Voices Ringing." The mood was different. The hymn encouraged the children to turn their thoughts to God. It is true that the children in that department did not sing "With Happy Voices Ringing" with the whole heart as they might have. This was because they were accustomed to the poor selection of a hymn intended to prepare for worship. In another department this same hymn was sung meaningfully because the boys and girls were used to having their hearts and minds always turned in praise to God at the beginning of worship, and they came to it with anticipation.

Leaders wishing to use hymns as aids to worship should see to it that they are fully aware of the distinction between hymns of praise, hymns of thanksgiving, hymns which call to worship, hymns about God, and hymns which address him directly in petition. The fact that a hymn mentions prayer does not make it a prayer hymn! Sometimes these types of hymns are mixed. "All Creatures of Our God and King," for instance, calls on sun and moon and all creation to praise God. But it has glorious "alleluias!" in which the singing children join in that praise.

- List hymns available for use in your church school department which address God directly in worship. Is there at least one stanza of those customarily used which does this? Write a simple hymn for the age group with which you work, making it a hymn of praise to God, addressing him directly. Write a hymn of thanksgiving. Unless you are fairly adept at writing poetry, your hymns may not be good enough to use, but they will help you to see the worth in the best of the hymns and

31

songs of praise available. Start a loose-leaf collection of hymns and songs from quarterlies and other current sources.

Quiet

A family group sat in the doorway of their tent home while a wonderful sunset filled the sky with glory. The mother murmured, "The heavens declare the glory of God, and the firmament showeth his handiwork." Then there was silence. In that silence the family worshiped.

A grandmother, almost totally deaf, sat at the table with the family. All heads were bowed, and in complete silence each offered his thanksgiving prayer. The members of the family had decided that since Grandmother could not hear the prayer and so be a part of it, they would offer thanks as she did, in the heart.

A school for the deaf gave a Christmas party to which some business women were invited. Part of the program was the singing of Christmas carols. Those who could hear a little sang. The rest enjoyed the rhythm which they could feel. One of the carols became for the visitors a moment of worship when completely deaf Arlene, in perfect time to the rhythm, interpreted "Silent Night" for her nonhearing companions with rhythmic movements of hands and arms and a lovely, tender expression on her face. In silence she found and helped others to find a moment of worship.

A kindergarten group sat entranced before a beautiful springtime picture. They had been for a walk and had talked of how God had planned for seeds and plants to keep alive during the winter. They had prayed in thanksgiving when they came back into their room. Now they were finding quietness their mode of expression.

In a primary group were children who had never attended a church before coming to the department. They broke into any attempt to worship with comments, questions, and the usual happy inconsequence of remarks. Nothing seemed to help them think of being in communion with God. Then one of the teachers suggested trying silence. She described to the children a time when she went to a Quaker church where there was no singing, no scripture reading, and no speaking except when someone felt guided by God to read or speak. The children were interested. She told of how everyone became very quiet; of how each one thought about God and his goodness; of how strong the feeling became that God was right there. "Would you like to try this way of being quiet?" she asked. The children did want to. For a period of weeks they entered into silence, at first, for just two minutes but finally, for as much as ten minutes. Then they were ready to sing praise to God whose presence they had acknowledged. They were ready to make an offering, to hear a story or scripture passage, and to join in spoken prayer. Meaningful quiet in which God's Holy Spirit might speak to them had guided them into worship.

● What use are you making of quiet? Is the quiet really quiet, and does everyone, including adults, cooperate in it? Do you give boys and girls the opportunity to let God speak to them instead of taking up every moment of the worship time with some voice or sound to which they must listen, or must join in producing? During the weeks that follow, at home, in class or departmental worship, in camp, before meals, and at other times, try a constructive use of silence. Be sure to explain at the beginning what the purpose of the silence is. Use some such statement as this: "As we are quiet, we think about God and open our hearts to him."

33

Centers of Attention

Consider two sanctuaries used for adult worship. Behind the pulpit of one (a modern structure) rise tier after tier of choir seats upholstered in red velvet. That church has a center of attention, but it is not one which helps the congregation into the mood of worship. The other is a very simple first unit, which the church will later use for educational purposes. Behind the communion table, a section of plain wood rises from the floor to the gable of the roof. A cross hangs there. To one side is a pulpit, and to the other, a lectern. Even without the cross, the pulpit, and the lectern, that unadorned panel carries the eyes upward and says, "Come and worship!" This center of attention holds nothing to divert thoughts, and so it becomes an aid to worship.

It is probably this principle to which heed should be paid—that children should not be diverted from giving attention to worship. Are they thanking God for Jesus Christ? Then a picture of Jesus may be a suitable; but not every picture. Those with a strong story emphasis will not aid worship, but will turn the thoughts of the children to the story. To create a satisfying and familiar setting for worship for older children, objects such as a cross or a Bible, candles or flowers may be arranged each Sunday. The question might be asked, "How well would adults worship in church if the pulpit furniture and the other appointments were drastically changed every Sunday?"

For young children, more variety is desirable. Their attention is caught by change, not by permanence, and they are sensitive to the mood of worship as they find it in the voice and attitude of the teacher. Young children worship easily when they are given opportunity. Yet, something of beauty, which helps them to forget the surroundings, is helpful at times.

- What centers your attention for worship at home? A family Bible with a beautiful cover? A table set for the meal, but with no distracting food yet upon it? What is there in your child's room? A little table with a Bible storybook? A small book of prayers? A picture of people praying? A Bible? A picture of Jesus? An illuminated prayer or psalm?

What centers attention for worship in your class corner or room, in your department? Does it say, "Come, let us worship together"? Does it center attention on worship, or divert it to other things?

Group Action

Certain things done by the group may of themselves aid the desire to worship. The recitation of a psalm in unison or the singing of a hymn may prepare for prayer. A choir number, either sung or in choric speech, may create a readiness for worship. If there is the slightest concert or program element in the presentation, it will be no aid to worship on the part of the listening group even if the performers do worship through it. Certain audio-visuals may be used successfully.

Talk of such things implies that leaders need to be keenly aware that for a group to recite a psalm in unison may be worship or it may be just a recitation. Subject matter does not constitute worship. In this connection, it should be recalled again that worship is a conscious opening of heart and mind to God. No matter what the lips say, if the heart has not turned to God, there is no worship.

A kindergarten manual suggested the use of the phrase "For every lovely thing, we give thanks to thee, O God." A simple but lovely melody was written for the words:

For every lovely thing,
For every lovely thing,
For every lovely thing,
We give thanks to thee, O God.

On walks in summer or springtime, the softly chanted refrain made worship possible as nature's beauties were encountered. It was used with pictures of everything, from a mother and child to blossoming trees. For an older group, it became a spontaneous response to beauty in a conference setting. In such a setting, singing was worship.

There are many values in using drama, choric speech, the work of a choir, audio-visuals. Because blundering can center the attention on the one who is speaking or the ones who are giving a drama or choir or choric speech number, rather than on God to whom the words are actually addressed, care needs to be taken. Sometimes these activities are worth while for purposes other than worship. Those who plan their use need to be sharply aware of whether the activity can lead to worship in a particular circumstance, fail to do so, or even prevent worship. Many things are worth while in their place, but that place is not necessarily in worship.

Because some part of the Bible is given in choric speech, there is no certainty that it becomes an approach to nor a part of worship. Unless the words are worshipful, it would be better to use them at some other time and for some other purpose. Much scripture is for instruction, clearer understanding, historical value, interpretation, and not for worship.

Any or all of these ways of securing group action may lead to worship if the words are right, the presentation is right, the time is right, and the mood is right. Only you can tell, as you watch your group and sense the reaction, whether what is being done is worshipful in reality, or is so only on the surface, going no deeper than the level of casual interest.

Atmosphere

Perception of the right moment and the establishing of custom may both make worship possible. For example, at a church dinner the best moment for table grace may be following the meal. In one church at family dinners the pastor has the blessing before the people file past the tables to fill their plates. Even the youngest child joins in the quiet moment of thanks.

At another church the plates are filled and then, while the sweet odors of hunger-stimulating food rise to nostrils, there is a pause for the blessing. The children, for the most part, have no part in that act of worship. They are too busy sneaking a bite, or being impatient at having to wait.

A junior class closes its study with prayer; it usually comes after the bell rings and the whole atmosphere is one of waiting to leap for the door. There is seldom any worship in the prayer. Another junior class begins with prayer. Sometimes it is worshipful and sometimes not. A third junior class has prayer at the time or times in the session when there is something to pray about, and its moment of worship usually is rich for all. If a teacher who follows this plan fails to find the right moment or the right approaches to prayer, then a set time may be better.

The one who is leading children so that their hearts increasingly open to God will sense the right moment and will accustom the pupils to worship in song and prayer at many times. That leader will provide children with ideas about God's nearness, his drawing them to himself at every moment of the day, and will help them to want to turn to God in awareness of his presence again and again as the hours go by. Habitude and atmosphere go hand in hand to help a child to moments of worship.

- Evaluate the group acts of worship of the children whom you lead. Try to work out in your mind what is leading them to worship, or preventing them from doing so. Decide whether these acts can, rightly handled, become aids to worship for your group, or should not be expected to do so. Work with some group act which should lead to worship but does not, and try to learn to handle it so that it does. Guide the group to use it as an approach to or as a part of worship.

  Consider some group act proposed for worship and decide for yourself whether or not it will result in worship. Exchange experiences with others to become more able to use, helpfully, these approaches to and parts of worship.

  Think carefully about the atmosphere and the custom of worship which you can detect or establish for the enrichment of boys and girls with whom you work.

It is a joyful thing to help children to want to worship. It takes skill to find the doorways that open hearts and minds to the eternal presence of God. It takes time, thought, experimentation, and sensitiveness of soul. It takes the help of God himself who has entrusted to parents, teachers, and friends the task of bringing his little ones to him.

Materials are an important part of any study. The following conversation might occur between persons who are considering materials.

Question: What materials are you using?

Answer: That depends on the age of the children with whom I am working.

Question: Why should that make any difference? I see young children in church worshiping right along with the adults.

Answer: You see them getting something and missing something. The minister's choice of materials is based solely on the needs of his adult congregation.

Question: My child gets a lot from it. I'm sure all children would.

Answer: When we think of materials for children's worship, we must think about what will contribute most to the child's growth and understanding. A child certainly might gain a little from a sermon related to adult problems, but he will gain much more from teaching related to his own problems as a child. He will understand something of what adults are praying earnestly for, but he will grow spiritually in a better way if he can pray about problems he, as a child, faces and in words he understands fully.

Question: Do you, then, advocate using only what a child at any age can completely understand?

Answer: No. Children need to stretch to new understanding. They need stimulation. They are able to use some things that are not quite clear to them, just as every adult may find in worship materials that which is not clear, not fully understood, but which challenges his best thought and grows in meaning as he grows in ability to understand. But materials for children must have a basis in the child's present life and understanding.

Question: Doesn't that limit the presentation of Christian truth?

Answer: A baby gets protein in milk; a man in meat. But in both cases it is protein. Christian truth applicable to a child's understanding is Christian truth no less. And if it be consistent with what is taught adults, it will form a basis for deeper understanding later on.

Question: Give me an example.

Answer: Take a simple song, "Dear Father for Thy Gifts to Me," No. 176 in *Hymns for Primary Worship.* That could be sung meaningfully by a five-year-old. Contrast "O Lord, We Praise Thee for Our Brother Sun," *The Whole World Singing,* page 14. It would take older primary or junior children to sing this with intelligence and understanding, yet one is an elaboration of the essential truth of the other.

- Look at two songbooks or hymnals used in your church, one with young children, the other with older boys and girls. Find something that expresses essential Christian teaching in a simple form, usable with a five-year-old. Then, find an expanded or more difficultly phrased expression of the same truth, which could be used with sixth-graders to expand their understanding and make use of what is expressed.

Exactly what is the hymn saying if you put it into prose? Is there anything in the simpler form which will have to be discarded because it does not agree with the truth in the more difficult statement? Is there a thought in your junior hymnal by which younger primary children could benefit if it were stated in simpler form? What other sources have you for hymns or songs to be used in your department? Look over any sources available to workers in other denominations.

Why Use Music?

Worship involves the will, the giving of oneself. Since music is an outpouring of self in emotion, it can be an effective aid to worship. As it is so used, remember that you may find that in actual practice music also has other values. As certain types of music play their part, you may find Henry, who is so unresponsive, suddenly quiet within himself, and thus free to open his heart and feel God near.

1. *Music Sets the Amosphere.* In one little country church with limited leadership, the pianist played "Nearer My God to Thee," with variations in almost jazz time and mood, as the introduction to worship. In another, the opening music was a display of what the organist could do in the way of combining her skill with all the variations of stops. Music can be

used to set entirely the wrong atmosphere as well as being used rightly. A new plan was tried in a Primary Department where it was very hard to get children, not accustomed to real worship, into a mood where worship was possible. The children were lined up at the back of the room as the pianist began to play a meditative lovely bit of music. This was the signal for quiet agreed upon with the children. When all was quiet, the leader moved forward and the children followed, going noiselessly to their places. Then the pianist played "O Come and Let Us Worship." The children sang it. They became quiet in mind as well as in body, and this is vital for worship whether it is spontaneous or formal.

The frantic cry to God which may come out of turmoil of mind is something else. It is of the essence of worship, but is not of concern just now. This chapter is concerned with the moods which music can induce, through which the child becomes more ready to set aside other thoughts and turn to God who is reaching out to persons.

These children, who at first had to sing this same hymn in hushed tones because they needed to have a sharp contrast to the way they had been singing, became able to sing joyfully and with full hearts, as befitting worship. They grew able to think of God in their worship as they had not before, and to feel themselves as a group responding to him in a way which was quite new to them. Every new child who entered the department was taken aside by one of the teachers and the customs of worship of this particular group were explained to him; and, what is more important, why there was silence before going to and during the time of worship. Thus each new child was helped to look forward to opening his heart to God in quietness and attention and readiness to feel his presence. It was a privilege to see such children smile in comprehension of the plan and go eagerly with the others to what was for some of them a new experience.

- What kind of music do you use to help create the mood for worship? Does it suggest quietness and devotion? Do the children understand the purpose of the music—to help put thoughts other than those about God out of mind—and do they assent to and cooperate in this use and purpose?

  Does the music actually help to set a mood in which it is possible to open the heart to God? If not, what can you do to change or improve the way the music is played, the attitude of the other adults, the attitude of the children toward its use?

2. *Music Adds Emotion to Intellect*. While the words of worship are very important in spoken prayer, music adds an emotional value to the thoughts already expressed. You have only to have a group read in unison the words of a praise hymn, and then have them sing it, to realize that there is additional value because of the music. Something has come into persons' lives with the abundance of color printing. Fifty years ago the color print was a treasure, for the process was expensive and most art work was reproduced in black and white. Think of television today. How much richer and more lifelike is color television than black and white. Music is something like that. It takes the black-and-white, accurate, vital truth and clothes it with something that adds poignancy to it. Children, deprived of music in their religious nurture, are being cheated of something that never can be replaced. Their lives will be the poorer forever because the quality that music can give to worship is not there.

- Turn to the loveliest music in the children's hymnal which you use with your particular age group. Read aloud the words set to this music. Then sing them. What difference do you feel? The next time you have opportunity, have the children read or repeat the words of this song in unison, then sing it.

Which do you think was most effective? Remember that you can use music for an emotional appeal with words that are silly, undignified, untrue, meaningless, and unworthy. This is not the sort of use and value of music that is being considered. Great and good words with worthy music are what is being sought.

3. *Music Itself Is Beauty.* Singing is one aspect of worship. Is it a virtue to offer ugliness to God? Remember the directions for the first tabernacle? In all the drabness of wilderness life, beauty flamed in the hangings and appointments of that movable place of worship. Anything less than the most beautiful would have been an insult to God. Later, the temple rose with such beauty that, after its destruction and a new place of worship was built, the old men who had known the former temple wept, remembering its beauty! Music can be beauty. If our worship of God is to be complete, we must offer our best effort to him. Inattentive or indifferent singing, "Let's see whether the boys or girls can sing loudest" singing, singing concentrated upon the singer is not worship partly because it is not beauty. It is bringing to God an unworthy offering in song!

A junior group sang very indifferently. The singing meant nothing to them and, one may assume, nothing at all to God to whom they were supposed to sing. A woman who felt strongly about music and its function in worship came as a teacher into that department.

She wondered what could be done to make the music true worship. Her solution was to work first at making it beautiful. She argued that until the juniors were singing in such a way that they were proud of it and felt its beauty, they could not make of their singing an offering to God. She concentrated upon their singing as one voice. This took attention, and listlessness vanished. She worked to have them sing softly, but meaningfully. This was helped by learning to understand the words and to speak them as if they were being addressed to someone. It took patience, but in time those juniors were singing hymns as hymns should be sung. Oddly then, there was no need to talk about singing being an offering to God of their heartfelt worship. Beauty became worshipful because it was worthy and because attention was concentrated upon it to the extent that the juniors found themselves freed to think of God as they sang.

- In numerical order, rate ten of the songs you are using regularly as to the sheer beauty of their music, melody, and harmony (if accompaniment is used). As a study group, mention what each person thinks is the most beautiful song used with the children and have these played and sung with attention to that point. Are there other songs available which are more beautiful, both in words and music (not forgetting that they must have integrity), but which you are neglecting because they are unfamiliar or you have not bothered to have the children learn and use them? Is the singing of your group beautiful, purposeful, and meaningful? If not, think over what you can do to help make it so. You will not stress these things with kindergarten children because you do not have formal worship with them, and they do not yet need to learn to make an offering of beauty in song. Their beauty is an unconscious one.

4. *Music Brings Out the Meaning and Gives Emphasis to Certain Words*. Perhaps this function of music can best be thought about by trying an experiment. Hymn tunes and song tunes have many different meters. That is, the length of line and emphasis is different in most tunes. Even when it is the same, a certain tune may not fit words that could be sung to it in the number of syllables in the line and number of lines. To wed music to words, there must be the right mood of the accompaniment and the words when read aloud. The emphasis provided by short and long notes must agree with the emphasis of the syllables as they are sung.

Think of these four lines of an opening stanza to be sung by juniors:

> Lord, as we gather in Thy house today,
> May we rejoice in all Thy love and care,
> And of Thy presence richly be aware.
> O be with us, and with us ever stay!
>
> G.W.M.

The meter is, 10-10-10-10, that is, ten syllables to each line.

How wed a tune to these words? Your adult hymnbook may reveal many 10-10-10-10 tunes. If you have never worked with this interesting procedure, find the Metrical Index, which gives the various meters and lists under them the numbers of the hymns and the names of the different tunes in that meter.

Try to find in that index (or in the Index of Tunes) the one called "Ellers." As you sing these four lines to that tune, you find that the syllables fit but the tune will not do. The long notes in the last line put the emphasis on the wrong words.

Now, find the tune "Eventide." That would fit but the mood is wrong. It is plaintive, while the four lines of verse should be positive. "Eventide" has no joy in it.

Turn to the tune called "National Hymn." It fits the words, but it is martial music and does not have the spirit of petition.

How about "Morecambe"? The mood is right for each line; the emphasis is right for line and word. The tune brings out the thought and gives emphasis to certain words. If it is sung in the right tempo, neither too fast nor too slow, and if the hearts of the juniors are in it, it forms a good piece of material for aiding worship.

- To become proficient in guiding children's growth through music, learn to handle meter and mood. Try having your group write a new stanza for a beloved hymn. Try writing a verse (a simple four lines). Now find a tune that fits it. Using the metrical and tunes indexes, find the tune which best fits it. Sometimes this will be difficult, especially if you write the verse and polish it before finding a tune. The writer once needed a hymn of praise, directly addressed to God, for the children of her Primary Department. When the hymn was finished, to her consternation, no tune but "Finlandia" would fit it! Interestingly enough, that tune which she considered much too hard for primary children was very easily learned and deeply loved by them. Children respond to worth and beauty and will worship best through them.

5. *Music Can Bring Individuals into a Group.* Happy group feeling comes with singing. A group of children singing around a campfire proves this. Communist tactics with youth in East Germany highlights what

group fervor can be roused by singing. A singing family of differing ages may have a unity that other families lack. Music is a powerful emotional factor in life, and its power should be studied and made fruitful in the Christian nurture of children.

Again, let it be stressed that only the best is good enough for worship. Start where you are, but seek always to find that which is of greater worth and greater beauty. Adults are tempted to use what they as children used and loved; but they need to remember that better and more helpful and really lovely songs and hymns are being written and composed all the time. Even though reluctant, they should abandon some of the old favorites in order to give the children a better medium for their most heartfelt approaches to God in worship.

- One primary group needed opportunity to learn hymns. They also wanted to have times when the children could sing just for the love of it. (These were not times of worship.) A teacher listed songs and hymns the children chose just because they wanted to sing them. One stanza each was the limit (unless some other child asked for the second stanza) so that more might have opportunity to choose. The children marked on a chart with single, double, or triple stars their estimate of how well they knew each hymn. Often, they worked at getting a one-star hymn into the two- or three-star class, "because we need to know it for our Thanksgiving worship," or some other reason.

Think about similar group singing for learning and for sheer enjoyment that you have had with children. How did it affect the group feeling? How can you use that feeling to improve the quality of your music? What steps might you take? Compare what you are doing with what other members of this study group are doing in the use of group singing for enjoyment, or to encourage singing that is meaningful for worship.

Why Use Pictures?

Pictures create atmosphere and give ideas as well. Pictures clarify situations. Pictures are usually things of beauty. Pictures concentrate attention. As pictures are thought of in relation to worship, there is, for the most part, a crossing of the borderline between pure worship and instruction, which may be a part of a "worship service." There needs to be made clear the distinction between the two functions which take place in times of worship.

Jenny is listening to the story of the lost sheep. She has no idea what a shepherd is. Pictures help her to know, and they clarify the story for her. Pictures help her to feel the lostness of the little lamb, the devotion and anxiety of the shepherd, and his joy when he finds it and brings it home. Scripture, retold for Jenny and clarified for her by pictures, may lead her to feel glad that the shepherd cared and found the lamb. It may lead her to want to thank God for those who help look after helpless things and keep them safe. Worship for Jenny is the prayer. It is not the story which she hears. It is not the pictures on which she concentrates. It is the prayer or the feeling of "thank you, God," which follows.

Remember that the main function of music is as an expression by the children, in hymns, songs, responses, and praise. This quality is not found in pictures shown to them, or looked at by them. When children are given a worshipful feeling through music, as when listening to "Silent Night, Holy Night," a sense of devotion is stirred which may be paralleled by a picture such as one of the first Christmas.

Where music may create atmosphere, as when the pianist plays something that brings the juniors' thoughts into quietness, it, too, may be paralleled in a picture. Coming into a room where a canvas conveys all that the artist felt in reverence, wonder, awe, or delight in God's world, may create the same mood in the juniors.

The main function of pictures is to draw forth an emotional response or to open the windows of the mind and heart and let the child see that which will make him want to worship.

● Think about the pictures you habitually use in worship with primary or junior boys and girls. Do you recall any one of these pictures which in and of itself gives a feeling of awe, reverence, or has helped the boys and girls to be quiet and center their thoughts on God? What experience of your own is related to some picture? In the weeks ahead, find lovely pictures of sky and clouds, sunset, or mountain majesty with a glorious sky above (*Arizona Highways* in the course of a year is a gold mine for such pictures) and mount one for each of your class members. Use these pictures in class with the verse:

The heavens declare the glory of God; and the firmament sheweth his handywork.

—Psalm 19:1, KJV

Let each child take home to place in his bedroom the mounted picture you prepared or that he has chosen from those you provided. Ask each child to learn and recite Psalm 19:1 while looking at the picture before he has his daily quiet time, and as often in the day as he thinks of it. A week later, ask whether saying the verse while looking at the picture has helped them to be ready to pray. Do not suggest to them when you give them the pictures, or at any time before, that you think the pictures may so help them. You probably will find that the children feel that the picture has helped. If so, you may be able to use pictures more fruitfully in your times with the boys and girls.

1. *Forms of Pictures.* For group use, pictures must be large enough for the entire group to see details easily. Large flat pictures are expensive, but a person can collect some gradually. For instance, a poster-size "Freedom to Worship God," by Norman Rockwell, is a treasure. A framed "The Omnipotent," found on sale in a picture store where many framed pictures were a dollar each, was something to be bought with appreciation. Copies of other good works of art sometimes may be found in similar situations. Denominational publishing houses have suitable pictures in sets, and have lists of other pictures and sources.

Too little use is made of slides to be used in an ordinary projector. Combinations of scripture, hymns, and slides in color, rightly chosen, can provide an opportunity in which worship may occur. Elsewhere, mention has been made of the response, "For every lovely thing," set to music simple enough for use with the very young child. A kindergarten teacher used it with her children on many occasions until they all sang it almost spontaneously as they looked at some lovely thing. Then she chose five or six slides, each lovely in itself: kittens, a mother and child, flowers, a waterfall, a baby of another land, meadows and sky—and showed them as the children sang again and again, "For every lovely thing, we give thanks to thee, O God." Pictures provided a widening of understanding and brought into the moment of worship a broader segment of life than the teacher could provide in actual experience.

Filmstrips are becoming more available. These are useful for informational background, especially for older children. Whether they can be used in worship depends entirely on their mood and what they stimulate in the mind of the child.

While informational material is often used in worship services, it does not necessarily lead to worship and might better be put into a "Let's-find-out-about" period, with the leader watchful for spontaneous worship.

● In what forms are you using pictures as aids to worship? In creating atmosphere? In suggesting what the thought of the day's worship is to be or in stimulating thoughts about which worship is to be centered? To what extent were the pictures you used this past week really a part of worship? To what extent did they clarify ideas so as to lead to more understanding worship? Were any of them informational, making no contribution to worship? Mentally, by going through your files, or by looking at pictures in an exhibit or in a store, decide which one would best be used to create a feeling of wonder that might lead to group worship.

What About the Scriptures?

Scriptures are used in worship. Not all scripture is designed for worship. Parts of the Bible are historical; parts are doctrinal; parts are worshipful; and parts are instructional.

Choosing scripture wisely for use in worship is one of the most difficult tasks that you, who are trying to improve your ability to guide children in worship, will have to face. If God is to speak to children through scripture, lean heavily on his guidance in choosing which to use with them. You will, of course, find excellent help in suggestions for worship scripture in the materials provided for use by your church. Sometimes the scripture suggested for study is appropriate for worship. At other times, it may be better not to use it. The worship service gives opportunity for use of scripture which relates the child's thinking directly to God. The study scripture for the day may relate to the child's own problem and center his thoughts on self.

● Think of a child with whom you work. Consider three scripture passages or verses which, for this particular child, will express wonder, awe, love of God, and praise to God. If you cannot think of these, you are not ready to lead in worship. Do not turn away from the need. With God's guidance, search the scriptures and find such passages or verses. You will find help for selecting scripture in the worship resources included in many hymnals. Other sources offering such guidance are the printed curriculum materials, the children's story papers, and worship books. Plan to learn by heart at least one of these each week, so that you will begin to possess scripture which can be used with your children. The use of such scripture, coming spontaneously from your heart, can lead to or enrich worship with your group. If, on the other hand, you have to stop to look up passages in a Bible, the vital moment will vanish, the mood and the opportunity will pass. More will be said in the chapter on resources about equipping yourself with scripture.

1. *Why Use the Scriptures?* Before you read further, try to answer this question yourself. List your reasons before you continue reading. This is a question you should always have before you, because, unless you are discerning, you may slip into the unfruitful use of scripture in worship. Part of your responsibility is to use

53

God's word rightly, not carelessly; not without thought. Think together about this. As a study class, you should have a considerable list of reasons for using scripture. Are the following reasons included?

Scripture is used because through the Bible God can speak to teachers and to children.

The Bible reaches heights of thought and utterance, under God's leading, that other words do not.

The Bible has authority.

God's nature and his concern for mankind is expressed in the Bible.

Words of worship, praise, contrition, soul-searching, delight, wonder, awe, love, repentance, and need are found there in a form that can be appropriate to each person's use.

The Bible contains teaching that can lead to understanding God's will and to a desire to follow it.

There is beauty in the phrasing of the Bible which helps worship.

There are many other reasons for using scripture in worship. Remember that not all scripture is designed for this purpose, but from scripture one can find resources to meet the need of the moment.

- There is to be a church picnic and in the lovely setting of a wooded park a brief period of worship is to be held before going home. You are on a committee to plan the worship. All age groups will be there—from young children to adults. Think of three types of scripture that will help that group to enter into the feeling that God is with them and that he rejoices in his children's happiness.

You are the member of a family, one of whose members is starting on a long journey. What scripture will you choose for family worship that morning?

Little Betty's puppy was run over today. Can your use of scripture at bedtime prayers help her?

Recall what has been said about the heart of worship. In what way has your choice of scripture in these three instances brought the children in the church group, in the family, and in individual cases such as that of Betty, to feel God's presence, his concern, and love?

Perhaps you chose scripture for some reason other than its value for worship. Scripture has many functions. What you need to learn is when it opens the heart to God, and when it is serving some other purpose in the Christian nurture of children. Betty may need to have her ideas straightened out through the use of scripture and a little conversation rather than having an experience of worship made possible at this particular moment. Just because this text is about worship, do not forget that the whole scope of Christian nurture is your responsibility, that worship is one part of it, and that you are equally responsible for its other functions.

2. *How Shall Scripture Be Used in Worship?* There are many, many ways of using scripture. Some are traditional. Not all of them are worshipful. Two ways are found in many churches, and often in children's departments, especially the junior, that are not worshipful. The responsive reading is designed to involve the total congregation in the reading. This breaking up of a scripture passage, verse by verse, often completely destroys any "feeling" about it. The group is more concerned with watching when to stop than in the meaning of what is being read! And the one who is thinking about what is being read too often finds him-

self reading with the leader after everyone else has stopped! If you doubt this, think about your most favorite story—the one that you love to tell the children—and imagine how effective it would be if you said one sentence and then they all said the next, you the following, and they the fourth, and so on. It would completely ruin the story! Just so does the responsive reading ruin the reading of the scripture, except where the congregation's part is a real response as in a few of the psalms.

The second misuse of scripture is observed when the inability of the reader comes between the words and the understanding of the listeners. There is a time for the children to read scripture verses, passages, and stories aloud. Unless they can do so in such a way as not to draw attention to themselves by blunders, self-consciousness, mistakes, mispronunciations, and inability to read, their reading will not result in worship for the group.

There is a place in worship, though, for reading scripture that will enrich or enlighten. Ordinarily, its connection with the rest of the worship service should be obvious. A primary group had been learning the lovely children's hymn, "Hushed Was the Evening Hymn." They had heard the story of Samuel. They had talked about how God can guide persons who turn their hearts to him, and who, as did Samuel, feel God's presence so vividly that it is as if an audible voice speaks to them. This, over a period of weeks, was training for worship. Then came the day when, as they gathered for their time of quietness and worship, the story of Samuel was the scripture passage read. It was followed by their singing the hymn. In the prayer lines of that hymn the children became very earnest, and one could sense that the vivid appeal of the story from the Bible had made them desire greatly God's guidance in their own lives. The scripture and the hymn together created an understanding that God can and does enter into people's lives to direct them; that even a child may count upon God's desire for his cooperation. With this strong feeling came the individual petition, even though it was voiced corporately.

The juniors in one group were helped to feel responsibility to do their part no matter how insignificant it seemed to them. The scripture read was a story of Jesus feeding the multitude when he said to his disciples, " 'You feed them.' " This led to a real sense of devotion as they offered to God their determination to meet their responsibility in a forthcoming offering with sincerity and concern for those whom they would help in this way.

● Think of a Bible story or teaching which you can tell or read to your children. In what way might this lead to a moment of worship, whether used in a planned service, in class, or at some other time? If you feel that it cannot do so, then try to think of some other story or teaching which would. Do not limit worship to praise of God. Remember that offering devotion, love, understanding, determination to do better, or many attitudes of heart and mind are or can be worship. The essential thing is that the child be aware of God and respond to his outreaching.

3. *Is Memorizing the Scriptures Important?* Kenneth was with a group of boys who were "just fooling around." In the course of their rambling, they came close to the fruit farm of an elderly man.

"He's had a heart attack," said one boy. "He can't chase us now."

The rest grinned. No one had to mention that the plum trees were loaded with ripe fruit.

But Kenneth, to his annoyance, found himself thinking, "You shall not steal."

"Oh, forget it," he said to himself impatiently. "There're more plums than anyone can use." But that deeply learned verse would not depart from his memory.

"Let's ask first," he suggested. Rather doubtfully the boys rang Mr. Jones' doorbell.

"Why sure!" said Mr. Jones. "The ones on the ground are ripest." He smiled. "I sure appreciate your coming to ask instead of just taking the fruit."

Kenneth and the boys raced out to the trees to feast. But Kenneth had a warm, happy feeling. He had been taught that through the words of the Bible God would guide him. He wondered a bit whether God had made him remember that verse just then, or whether it had just happened. But he felt a kinship with God in doing what he knew was God's way.

Memorizing meaningful scripture verses and passages very often can open the way for God's direct guidance. When this is acknowledged, there is a feeling of communion, of having been in harmony with God, that is worship, whether in a group or as an individual.

Learning passages to be used in informal or formal worship is very worth while. Just as a hymn sung without the intervention of a printed page or chart can come from the heart, so can the scripture passage. However, such a passage must be true to a child's experience. He must not be avowing sentiments that no child can have.

- What verses have the boys and girls in your class memorized lately? In what ways (discussion, picture, story, conversation) have you made them clearly applicable to the child's world, understanding, and daily life? Think of a circumstance in which you would hope that one of these verses might be used of God to guide a child in the right way. Do you know of one instance of such guidance? Have you had any experience yourself of having guidance through scripture you recall, whether you have memorized it, or just are very familiar with it?

Have you ever tried having the children work out and pose "pictures" interpreting biblical teachings for their age and times, taking colored pictures to lend importance to their ideas, and showing these as they recall such verses?

Have you accustomed the children to turn to God in thanksgiving for his guidance as they think and talk about it?

Check over the passages you are having the children learn. Can each child say these words without perjury? Or is there a chance that some child may be rebelliously saying inside himself, as Kerry did, "I haven't done anything so horrible that I need to pretend to God that I have!" when a psalm that rose out of deep conviction of sin was imposed upon a junior group for learning. For juniors to learn some things in their right historical relationship is quite different from learning them as material practical for the juniors' own approach to God.

There is so much that can be used in worship if the words come from the heart as we come close to God. All the things which have been mentioned—music, scriptures, pictures, and many others—may lead to worship. The task is to be sure that what is chosen with the help of God does enable a child to become conscious of God's presence and to have communion with him. Nothing should be taken for granted, but watched to find out whether, in reality, the materials are opening the doors of opportunity to the boys and girls. Through them they should find the joy of praise, prayer, comfort, and help in the presence of God; be led to a greater desire to do his will; and led to commit their lives to his guidance and direction.

4.
Some Principles of Worship and Its Language

When the heart overflows and speaks to God, responds in praise or in urgent petition, one may be tempted to say that there is no principle involved. Yet, there is a basic truth which is at the heart of worship. That is the awareness that God is, and that he is within one's consciousness.

This chapter will not deal with this basic truth or principle. It will consider techniques which leaders can use as worship is planned for and with children. Worship is planned in the hope that certain materials, actions, and thoughts will lead the boys and girls to open their hearts to God and respond to him in love.

There is sequence to what is done or what the children are asked to do. God is praised by thankful persons who feel humble in the presence of such greatness and glory. They contrast their inadequacy with his competency, their failure with his goodness. Penitence follows, with the realization of having fallen short of God's will, and there is petition for forgiveness, help, and guidance. God's forgiveness is accepted and a desire to walk in his way surges within. After listening to an admonition, a sermon, a story, a talk, this desire is expressed in the giving of an offering, a declaration of loyalty, dedication, or belief. The worshipers are secure in God's keeping and receive a blessing before they leave the hour of worship.

This is not to say that every service of worship carries its participants through this sequence of experience, nor that hymns, scripture, prayers, and other elements are likely to do so. Even in adult services of worship, many ministers or leaders fail to observe the sequence or rise to the climax of worship in which lives are consciously aligned with God's will. Where this sequence is ignored, with no consideration of the fact that it is the natural way in which people respond to God's loving outreach, persons are less likely to have an experience of being close to God.

Liturgical churches do not have this problem. The sequence of thought in coming into full recognition of God's presence and will has been predetermined through years of experience in the way in which minds move.

Nonliturgical churches need not feel that only through a set liturgy may they come into God's presence. They do need to understand and to apply the principles of progression of thought and emotional involvement in worship. Such understanding will help persons more readily find the opportunity to worship.

Those who guide children into experiences which may make worship possible for them, cannot ignore the fact that thought can be led onward toward God, or can be broken off. This can be worse than if the process had never started.

- Consider a church bulletin or your planned junior or primary worship service for last week, and compare its items with the progression of thought given above. Remember that seldom is the whole gamut of experience touched, although it may be. In children's worship it would be limited, although it is surprising what the introduction to a hymn or the words of a prayer can include in short and simple terms.

In your time of worship for children, how much attention has been paid to progression? Or is it haphazard, based on choosing hymns children sing well, or those which they like, or those with the titles or first lines which fit a theme selected for the day?

You may be puzzled about how to apply progression to a worship service prepared in advance. Here are some examples:

Mrs. Jones surveyed the primary children who were busy with paste and scissors. "O come and let us worship," she began to sing. Then louder, "O come and let us worship," Then still louder, "O COME AND LET US WORSHIP!" By the time she had sung this three times, most of the children were gathered in chairs facing a poster of animals. Mrs. Jones began to talk about animals the children knew.

NOTE: (1) There was nothing leading the children to quiet when they might have moved from what they were doing to the chairs in a completely informal "processional," imitative of the way in which people entered the temple courts as individuals to worship, or as they come by families into the sanctuary. (2) The call was a signal for quiet and assembly, not for worship. A buzzer would have done just as well, if not better, for the call to worship was misused. Why? (3) No worship or sign of it followed the leader's saying to the children, "O come and let us worship God our Lord!" How could these children worship God—become quiet in his presence and think about him or sing his praise—while talking about all the elephants, donkeys, and kittens they had known? Being quiet in God's presence is preliminary to thinking about God and can be the very highest form of worship. One of the psalmists recognized this and included in his song of praise what he, in his heart, heard God say: " 'Be still and know that I am God,' " (Ps. 46:10).

Mrs. Benson watched carefully as the children were busy with their various activities. When they were nearly through, she signaled the pianist to play a quiet, meditative piece. The children who had finished moved quietly to the chairs set for them, facing a low table with a lovely springtime picture of blossoms, sky, and hills. They listened to the music and looked at the picture as the others soon came to join them. Then all sang together, "O come and let us worship." When they had finished, Mrs. Benson said simply, "I am going to tell you a story this morning," and then began.

NOTE: (1) The place of worship was attractive, simply arranged, and helped to create the right mood. It had something for the children to enjoy in quietness as they gathered. (2) The music was without words, so was used rightly to create mood rather than to recall known ideas. (3) The children themselves sang what was proper, since the call to worship was designed in this instance to include all. (4) At this point Mrs. Benson failed. The children were in a receptive mood, the place was well designed, the call to worship had been given. But no worship followed! The children were given no opportunity to respond to God's outreaching love with expressions of praise, thanksgiving, or love directly addressed to God. There was no opportunity to sing about God nor to pray to him. Mrs. Benson led them to the point where they might have felt close to God, then abruptly concentrated attention on herself and her story. Without intending to do so, Mrs. Benson was using all that went on to get them ready to listen to her, not to enter consciously into the presence of God.

When this is done at the beginning of a time of worship, during it, or at its end, the materials of worship are misused. If "O come and let us worship" is not followed by the opportunity to worship, the meaning of the words becomes dulled. In fact, it ceases to have any meaning at all for the children. This kind of experience accustoms children to say, "Let's worship," then gives the feeling that a really exciting story ought to follow! Anticipation of worship should be followed by worship. When the word "worship" is used, no leader should fail to open the doors for it.

Someone is sure to say, "But you cannot make children worship. It does not follow that they will worship if you have the call to worship precede an act of worship." That is quite true. No one can guarantee that children will worship even when given every opportunity. But this can be guaranteed: Children will not worship when their attention is called to something other than God and his loving outreach toward them; when they are given no opportunity for responding to him!

If children are to worship, planning is important. The purpose may be defeated by ignoring the sequences of thought processes which will open the doors of worship for the boys and girls.

• Considering only the opening of your planned times of worship, go through the last three in which you have been involved either as a planner or as a worshiper with the children. What did the place and its arrangement say to the children? How were they brought into quiet so that withdrawal from thoughts of themselves was possible? Exactly what followed? These four things should have had a close relationship. Did they?

Instead of opening with worship, you may have planned for fellowship to come first. In that case, were any materials of worship misused? And when you did come to the high moment of worship, what was the sequence which led to it?

This is very difficult, someone may say. Of course it is! Guiding children into worship is not easy. If you pay attention to sequence, you will find that it becomes easier and is a delight to work toward achieving. The children will worship more easily and come to times of worship with a greater sense of the worth of what they are doing. This will make it more rewarding than anything you have ever done.

Think about any group where it seems best not to use an opening as formal as the call to worship with its following praise. In some cases children may not be ready in this short time to turn their thoughts to God. Keep constantly in mind that children are not to be forced into a given pattern. Rather, use your skill to help them to be ready for the quiet and the awareness that makes response possible for them.

Due to a rigid place-and-time situation, Peter Knowland, working with a group of juniors in a vacation church school, had to plan for worship to be directly after their recreation period. They were hot, some of them tired, boisterous, and in anything but a worshipful mood. Peter decided that fifteen minutes of "going through the motions" would be less desirable than five minutes of heartfelt adoration. So he planned accordingly. He had made himself a good storyteller. With a carefully chosen story, which had a direct relationship to the problems the juniors were facing, he led the group into unity, rested them, and laid a foundation for part of the worship he had planned.

Peter also used singing. He worked out a relationship between the story and the song. For example, a story of a daring colporteur who took Bibles to a South American Indian was followed, after a brief pause, by the remark, "You know, I never used to realize how lucky we are to have the Bible without any trouble at all. And I've come to think that the words of that song, 'Book of Books, Our People's Strength,' are very good. Let's sing it." They did.

Peter called attention to the last stanza, said a word or two about God, and suggested a hymn of praise to God. Then he spoke about the second phrase of the last stanza and suggested that they pray through the hymn, "Father, Hear the Prayer We Offer."

These choices had sequence and connection. They did not rise to a climax of worship, but they opened the way to several different moments of worship. Instead of using the prayer hymn, Peter might have suggested, if his group was used to doing so, that several juniors pray short prayers thanking God for the Bible in which they could find his will for their lives; or he could simply have suggested that they pray, speaking to God of whatever they chose.

One need not expect children to follow any sequence of thought in prayer in this instance. They may or may not. Who is to say, when a child is speaking to God, what he is to speak about? If what was planned has guided him into the moment when he feels God close and is ready to open his heart to him, what the child wants to say to God is his own affair.

- With your children in mind, think about and plan a sequence of the materials of worship that you could use at a campfire, in a vacation church school, or in a week-day church school situation. First, note the situation from which the children will come to the moments of planned worship. Decide what transition to use. Then, work out the sequence by which you will guide them to order their thoughts to become free to sense God's presence and be ready to respond to him. Remember that even after the most prayerful preparation on your part, there may be a time when the children just cannot achieve inner quiet.

Alice and Judy, two ten-year-olds, were so overcome with giggles one day that the leader wisely said, "Let's not try to have our worship time now. God wants us to be happy and laugh and have a good time, but we can't be doing that and think about him in the way we want to in our worship service. Instead, we'll sing some of the songs about our happy world and how we like to act in it."

There was no feeling of anger or disappointment in the statement, and the children soon were singing songs different ones chose. Alice and Judy giggled during the first one, but since no one was being shocked, the incentive to continue being silly was gone, and soon the two girls were singing heartily.

After one child had chosen and they had sung a prayer hymn, the leader felt the time and mood were right and said, "Would some of you like to ask God to bless our happy times together and thank him for what you especially want to?" Worship on this day, you see, depended on abandoning the carefully worked out plans and gave the children the much richer experience of coming to realize that one does not enter into worship irreverently, but prepares oneself to be ready for praise or prayer.

Suppose that in what you just worked out, some child or some circumstance filled everyone with the giggles. What would you do? How would you use that moment to help the children gain a better idea of worship? Think of three possible actions.

Something was said earlier about the way a hymn is introduced, or an idea is included in a prayer. The one who plans sequence in worship, so that the thought of the worshiper is led forward and upward, often has very clearly in mind the reason for choosing a passage of scripture, a hymn, or the wording of a prayer. Too often, this connection is in no way apparent to the children. It may be so nebulous that no one catches it!

"We have just sung 'O Worship the King,'" said Mrs. Lewis, "and we have spoken to God about his wonderful world. These are the words of a psalm in which the writer was thinking, just as we have been, about God's wonderful world." She read a section from Psalm 104. Then she said, "Now we are going to see a few pictures of some of the glories of God's world that are around about us. If you wish, you may join me in singing 'For every lovely thing,' as we look at the pictures."

Mentally picture that hymn, followed, without comment, by the scripture, followed, without any connecting remarks, by the pictures and the thanksgiving response. How barren the use of those three bits of worship materials might have been in comparison to what it was when a thoughtful connection was established.

This text is not designed to lay down a single way of planning and carrying out opportunities for worship.

It is designed to present ideas that have proven helpful, and to stimulate you to think your way toward the solution of any situation which may be a problem. Someone may say, "But I don't want to have everything connected up. I want to be able to hop, skip, and jump." Such a one should be answered, "Your concern is that your children be led by what you and they are doing together to the moments when they feel God close. The concern is not how lustily they sing, how glibly they recite a psalm, whether they enjoy a certain hymn, how much they look forward to a story, or how smoothly the planned order of service goes. Your job is to learn to sense whether or not you and the children, but particularly the children, are feeling a special closeness to God; whether they are shutting out thoughts of self, of excelling others in performance, or of any other thing which can stand between them and God and are finding themselves in communion with him. If they are not, no matter what you have planned, they are not worshiping."

It is your responsibility to find out, to give time to thinking out what it is that brings your children to the moment of worship. If spontaneous worship is the path for them, then you should use planned worship procedures in a limited way. If you do use planned worship procedures, remember that the mind works in certain ways. Be sure that you are going up a path; that you are not preparing a maze with ever-recurring dead ends.

• If you work with kindergarten children, select any song such as "In My Little Garden Bed" (*Finger Plays*, by Emelie Poulson), "It's Raining Today," "Friends! Friends! Friends" or some similar song which does not especially relate to God, and plan the sequence following it which might lead to a moment of worship. What sequence of comments, remarks, or encouragement to conversation will you plan to guide the children to worship?

If you work with primary children, plan a simple service for a morning of the first snow, of springtime, or of some special experiences; or look at one or more services which you have already planned and used. How is thought guided by your sequences? If it isn't, arrange it so that it will be. What brief connecting comments can you make to help the children move smoothly along the pathway toward worship?

Do the same for a worship service planned for juniors. If you are helping juniors to learn to plan their own worship services, what can you do to help them to see the need to move in sequence from one thought to another? What happens when worship moments are over?

In one department, Mrs. Close begins a vigorous and gay composition upon the piano. Why should she not?

In one junior camp, the children go silently to their tents after vespers. In another, they talk quietly around the campfire after a few moments of silence. In another, they are quiet for a moment or two, then, as the spirit moves them, get up and go happily off to bed, usually not making too much noise. Can you see advantages to all these plans, each in its place?

The primary and junior children of one public school came together for weekday worship and classes in a nearby church—all coming at one time and with volunteer teachers. A worship service closed the hour. Teachers and pupils alike were listening for the buzzer, which meant they barely had time to get back to the school for the next class. What did this ending do to worship? What would you have arranged instead?

71

In another weekday situation, the classes came one at a time to a trained teacher in a nearby church. The transition from school to church was very abrupt. What beginning and end would you have planned for a time of worship?

In a regular Sunday morning church school, a five-minute warning buzzer sounded at the end of the hour. Some classes broke loose then, some waited for the second buzzer. What would you have arranged to make the ending of worship effective?

● As you have answered each of the questions above, you will have seen that there is need to plan departure from worship as well as for entering into it. Think it over.

A few words should be said about the language of worship. Many years ago, even a very young child learned to pray, using "thee," "thou," "thy," and "thine" with the appropriate verb forms. In written form, the initial letter of each of these words was capitalized.

Then came a time when one school of thought was that a child would pray more naturally using "you" and "yours" as the terms of address to God. At the same time, the captial letters of these words were, for the most part, removed.

The other school of thought was that the older form of address to God should be retained; and in making this change, children lose more than they gain. It was reasoned that at the very time when children were learning easily and rapidly and adding new forms, new words, new meanings to their vocabularies, eight or ten reverent forms of pronouns and verbs would not be too difficult for them. At a time when they were learning social usages, and the different modes of addressing different members of the family, friends, and acquaintances, they needed to learn the mode of addressing God which would put him on a different plane.

There was another element in the reasoning of the first group, which, to the second, seemed strange. As children read or memorize portions of the Bible, they become familiar with these same forms without which they were supposed to worship better. Many hymns also use these forms and would lack a great deal in feeling and reverence if they were not used.

Guiding children in worship necessitates making them able to take part in group worship as leaders, and to express themselves easily in the language of worship. It seems to this writer that probably everyone needs to be able to understand and to use correctly the words "thee" and "thou," with the accompanying verb forms, as a lovely acknowledgment of reverence for God, and to be as unselfconscious about the use of them as when using "I," "my," "mine," "am," "do," and any other form of the first person singular.

There is an additional value in the use of the reverent forms of the second person singular, as applied to God, which is lacking when we train children to use only the common usage of today for personal communication. Akin to this question of the growth of the child in use of the reverent form is the need to guide him to use rich words in communion with God. The adult who always prays, "Our Father," or "Our God," is voicing one understanding of God. Why not use "Eternal God," "Gracious Father," "Lord of all being," "Mighty and Everlasting Lord," "Thou who art the Creator," and many other names by which God may be called as he is seen in the multiplicity of his Being? Tad's "Heh, you up there, God," is a far cry from the equally fervent cry to God which that three-year-old will utter as a twelve-year-old boy. Unless we guide children to use the many names of God and to rejoice in "Lord of the sunlight, Lord of the starlight, Lord of the seasons," their ability to think of God in terms commensurate with his greatness, goodness, and love will be impoverished.

● Think of children the age of those with whom you work and list as many different, suitable, mind-enlarging, devotion-expressing terms for God as possible that could be used by those children in prayer. Do you, in your own prayers, acknowledge in your salutation of God the many, many relationships he bears to you, to others, and to his world?

As a rule, prayers are not the place to tell the children what you want them to know, under the guise of telling God what he already knows. Certainly, it is no part of worship to take a slap at a child by such a prayer as, "Dear God, we're sorry Stanley didn't cooperate and so our program was spoiled. Help him to be more responsible in the future," or others of a similar nature.

What of the place of slang, current-word usage, and colloquialisms in prayers, and in the short talk in worship? Private prayer is one thing; as a child feels in his heart he should pray. When he earnestly prays his individual prayer in public, he may appropriately use the language with which he feels happy and at home. But part of growth in ability to take part in or to lead public worship is to learn to add dignity to sincerity, and to use words in which others can worship as well as words in which the leader himself can worship. If a worshiper tends to giggle as Johnny offers a prayer in the junior worship time, then Johnny is not succeeding in centering the thoughts of all on God. He gradually can learn to do so as he learns to employ language which will not be a stumbling block and will not call attention to itself instead of to God, to whom it is addressed.

• There are many lovely poems, hymns, prayers, and worship thoughts written for children. Do you have at least one collection to think about, to choose from, and to let the children ponder over? Such a collection is especially helpful for those old enough to want to compare and choose prayers to learn, hymns to sing, poems to memorize, prose extracts to copy or use, bits of beauty in language of worship to illustrate. You always will have to evaluate any collection of materials for use with children because it is your responsibility to teach the truth as you understand it. No matter how lovely a prayer to the Virgin Mary, a Protestant worker with children will not use it. No matter how attractive an idea, a conscientious worker with children will not use it if it departs from truth.

If you do not have resource books, are you using denominational materials which are rich in worthwhile, helpful ideas clothed often in beautiful language?

Before you go on to the next chapter, locate for yourself some source of enrichment in language that will increase the word power of children in worship, and plan how to use it with your group. If you are already doing this, do not weary in new research!

A special need is to help children to read the words of scripture accurately, meaningfully, and without stumbling. A church member who read loudly in the responsive sentences at the opening of the service, "Your Lord resigns!" while everyone else was reading "Your Lord reigns!" was losing the meaning of the triumphal assertion for himself and distracting everyone around him. One fine senior boy reads scripture passages so fast that no one can understand a word. From the time they read at all, children can be helped to read Bible verses, stories, and teachings in such a way that they themselves get the full meaning. Such reading also makes the words of the Bible something which has richness, beauty, and meaning for everyone who hears them.

Worship is too high and holy—too intimate and lowly —to approach it with anything but our best. In the best, one may walk in the beauty of orderliness and in a straight path, through loveliness, to the presence of God and thus into communion with him.

5.   *Worship at Home*

Worship in the home is vastly important. No other factor so deeply influences a child. It may begin with a mother kneeling by her baby's crib and praying, long before the child is really conscious of what is going on.

Margaret Alice Huggins in her book, *The Red Chair Waits,* gives a picture of two babies of China. One is in a home where the infant meets only rebuffs and scoldings. Even his mother does not dare comfort him after he has been slapped by the grandmother. He is a subdued, silent baby. The other child is surrounded by love. He laughs and jabbers and expects the world to love him. The two babies show a direct response to two different relationships with adults.

When worship is a part of the family environment from the very beginning, the young child absorbs the atmosphere and senses that his parents are finding a Presence beyond themselves to whom they give reverence.

- Think about your childhood background, your present family life, or some family with whom you are very intimate. What moments, customs, materials, or other factors said or say in that home, "We are a Christian family. We love God and worship him." Take time in making this list. Be ready to add to it at the close of this chapter.

Think of the possibilities of worship in the home in several different forms. Do not forget that there is a negative as well as a positive side to this matter. What is said and done may destroy a sense of worship or may develop wrong understandings. Worship at home is no easier to guide than is worship in any other place.

Times of Prayer

1. *Times for Prayer.* The time and place for private prayer are very important. A good illustration of this is one family that never failed to have family worship. The children felt real joy in it, but when the two older girls left home for college, they had no experience of carefully nutured private devotions to take the place of family worship and they quit any form of worship in private.

Norma felt things deeply. She had tried to set for herself a time for private devotions, but her mother's insistence upon knowing exactly what she was doing at all times, and her own shyness about saying that she was reading her Bible soon put an end to her attempts.

In another family the mother had bedtime prayers with the young children. It was a rich experience for them, but the moment they became able to put themselves to bed, the stern command, "Now let's see how fast you are into bed with the lights out," resulted in a muttered prayer too often cut short by dropping off to sleep. Soon there was a formal, stiff, and short supplication, or no prayer at all.

In one family the mother set aside a half hour following lunch for her own private devotions. The child who dared to interrupt was treated courteously, but made to feel like an intruder and was dismissed. "No," said one of these children, meditatively, when she was grown, "I can't recall a single time when any of the five of us, in all our childhood, were encouraged to have a quiet time alone with our own Bible storybooks, or were helped to plan for a time when we would pray."

Some families, on the contrary, do plan for such times. "I feed the children regularly," said one mother, "and it is just as important to establish a time for Bible reading and prayer." A father, even though tired from a long day at physical labor, took time every so often to be sure that his junior boy was developing in his ability to use the time set apart at bedtime to think over his day and talk to God about it. The companionship of his father in those moments gave the boy a deeper appreciation of the privilege, and a sense of the importance his father placed upon the custom.

So often these times of private devotion are not considered vital. Often they are more so than the so-called family devotions, which have an important place but should not displace, for any one of the family, the need for an individual approach to God.

● If you are a parent, think about this matter of encouraging your children to plan time for private devotions and how you may help them. If you have no children, think about your own practice in this regard. Think how you might help parents to plan for the same thing. Other suggestions in this chapter about private worship will give further ideas.

Consider also what happens when you have visiting children in your home. Do you take for granted that all home customs will be set aside while they visit you? Or do you consult the parents as to their customs and help the visiting children feel your kinship with them in desiring to be close to God by making a time and place for private devotions possible? How could you do so?

2. *Grace at Meals.* This is perhaps the easiest to establish of all the times of prayer. But wait! Does it occur only "when Dad is home," as Kevin remarked; or, as in one family, only when there are guests? Is it a mere formality conducted by a parent?

Grace at meals is opening the heart to God only if the hearts of all present are in it. The old English form, which the children of a family were supposed to offer in unison as they stood after a meal,

"For what we have received,
    May the Lord make us truly thankful!"

was hardly that. It suggests not thanks to God, but a hope that even though the food was not much, one could learn to be thankful for it!

Any set form used or mumbled before a meal fails to rank as worship. But grace at meals need not be so. It can be rich toward God!

Taking turns at returning thanks may include four- and five-year-olds. Six-year-old Patricia showed that it was a time of real prayer for her when she bowed her head one day and prayed,

"God is great and God is good,
    And we thank him for the trees. Amen,"

adding hastily to her startled mother, "I couldn't thank him for the food, Mother, when there were *beans* on my plate!"

80

Unison prayers are helpful before meals. Every family should practice silent prayer. There are many occasions when those trained to silent giving of thanks will be able and eager to do so, while those to whom grace at meals means spoken prayer simply will omit it. Silence also affords opportunity for each to offer his own thanks which may be much more prayer than when listening to a father or mother offer it.

Grace at meals may be varied in form. One father offers a real prayer that goes far beyond thanks for food. But he is wise enough to limit himself to a very short utterance when time or tempers are short.

There are many excellent graces which may be learned and used in unison or as individual prayers. Sometimes a family studies and chooses between two such graces, deciding which one best expresses what they want to say. Some may feel that memorized prayers are not advisable; but such prayers give growing children an experience of the richness of thought and language that can make even a short prayer memorable. They also may help children in voicing praise to God. A leading citizen of the United States still mutters the ten words of the most inadequate "grace" that can be imagined just because he was not helped as a child to feel thankfulness in more effective wording and varieties of grace. On the other hand, there is a woman in one church who often is called on for extemporaneous prayer at times when no one is prepared, and something very special is needed. She is able to voice, beautifully and adequately, the feelings of all. She says, "I have read, studied, and thought about the great prayers of the ages, and they have enriched my ability to pray." She never is hampered by feeble language but lets what everyone is feeling pour forth in prayer to God.

● Formulate a grace for a four-year-old to use; for an older child. What would you suggest a child remember as he prepares to represent the family in his turn at saying grace?

Find some sources in the church magazines of your denomination for short prayers suitable for children to learn or to use as examples. What forms do you use?

Listen carefully for the next few months to the table graces offered at church suppers, in family homes, and at public dinners. Are they really worship? Or are they mouthings of conventional form? Are they halting and stumbling, or do they show experience and habitual ease in addressing thanks to God?

Ask some of those who seem most able to lift the hearts of all in thanksgiving how they prepare for this responsibility in worship. Determine three ways in which your ability to make any grace you offer a real coming into the presence of God for all those for whom you speak.

3. Prayers at Special Times. Bedtime prayers, grace at meals, family worship, private devotions—all may take account of special events. These may include the birthday morning; the operation June is to have; the sad news of Grandmother's death; the visit of a dear friend; the start of a new job for Jim; the first day of school; the tough exam ahead and any other occasion which is significant. Sometimes a special prayer for one special thing may be expressed, as when John's father dropped in to sit on John's bed just before his first venture in camping out. The two of them prayed together, simply and briefly, asking God's presence, blessing, and guidance during the happy days ahead and asking him to be with the family at home, too.

- Think of ten coming occasions in your family or in the families of children in your charge in church school such as camp. Think of ways and times in which you can help children turn naturally to God in thanks or petition related to the occasions.

4. Prayers Brought Home. Often, children bring home something in the way of a prayer. This may be a litany, a prayer composed in class or camp, a prayer in their Sunday church school paper, one typed out and used in vacation church school or camp. Robert brought home a simple prayer for use before meals that his group had used in camp. He suggested that the family use it at home. His parents were sensitive to Robert's feelings and so, although they had never in their lives had any sort of prayer in the home, they followed his lead. Grace at meals became their practice. Too often, families brought up in the church tradition are not as thoughtful. They make no place in the family for prayers brought home. Most families could improve their performance as Christian guides for their children at this point.

- As a parent, do you keep what the children bring home and plan for its use, either as a family, at special times with the child, or in his private devotions? Do you post the prayer he brings home as prominently as his drawing from public school? Do you delight in the prayer he and his classmates worked out as you do in the short story he wrote in public school?
  As a teacher, are you helping parents to make use of what is going to the home? Can you find an interested parent who is doing so who will help other parents of children in your class to make use of what is sent home

to the glory of God and the enrichment of your pupil's lives?

Is what you are sending home worthy of use?

5. *Family Worship.* Family worship involves more than prayer; but think of it in connection with prayer because this is one essential part of it.

Establishing and maintaining family worship is for most families a most difficult thing. But so are many other vital parts of life difficult. If the difficulty is admitted, one is on the road to solution.

One way is to enlarge the scope of the grace at meals. If that custom is already established, the family may discuss the desirability of family worship. This will help children, especially older ones, to adjust to the idea of taking more time at the meal deemed best suited for a greater expression of appreciation to God. With only young children in the family, both the father and mother may make bedtime a prayer time and family worship, rather than just supervision and guidance of the child's worship. A family may start by finding some one thing each day around which brief worship may be built: a special occasion, something brought home, a need learned about, thankfulness for the day's opportunities, or petition about the day's difficulties. The possibilities in richer worship will be considered later.

● As a parent, do you have family worship? Is it a time looked forward to by all? Do you take time to prepare so it will be a lovely experience?

Using the Bible

1. *Honoring the Bible.* It used to be that the Bible, a huge imposing tome, had the place of honor on a table with a special drape beneath it. Today there are

other ways of honoring the Bible. In one family the now familiar red copy of the Revised Standard Version has a beautiful tooled leather cover in a delightful shade of blue. Wherever the Bible is placed—on the breakfast table, a shelf, a table in the living room—it is placed carefully, with nothing over or under it. That Bible is being used to the glory of God and its special covering shows it is a special book.

Another family has the custom of giving a place of honor on the walls of illumined portions of scripture—suitable passages such as the Lord's Prayer or the Shepherd Psalm. This family would place on a specially prepared background the scripture passages brought home by its children. These need not, and should not, stay up for long, especially if they are the efforts of young children which older boys and girls will not enjoy, or of older boys and girls which mean nothing to younger members. Often, Christmas cards and others have beautifully illumined or illustrated verses from the Bible. They may go on the family bulletin board as normally as any other message for the members to note.

• What place does the Bible have in your own home, or your room? Would any stranger coming in know that you and your family have and cherish a Bible? In homes that you visit, which is given most importance: the latest novel from the library, the newspaper, the various magazines, or the Bible? Why?

If a family is to witness to its faith; if the children are to know that the Bible is God's word and held in honor, what plans can you, your family, the families of your pupils deliberately make to honor it? Do something constructive along this line this week. Suggest to yourself several ways in which members of your church may be encouraged to show honor in their homes to the Bible as

God's word. Perhaps there is a class of young parents who need to think about this as they begin patterns of family response to God in their homes.

2. The Scripture in Many Forms. A family, devoted to the church, had two bookshelves full of expensive and delightful books for their two-year-old. Many were far beyond her comprehension, but she would grow into them and she already loved the pictures. Not one of the books had any religious significance. It is not easy to find such books even though the religious bookstores are full of them. Illustrations may be limiting to thought, but there are those which can be chosen and used with young children to good advantages, even though care must be taken to enlarge the visualization as the children grow older.

In another family, Bible picture books and storybooks, carefully chosen, were not only on the children's bookshelves along with their other books, but were used in family worship from time to time. One family, with four children ranging from three to thirteen years in age, loved the times spent with a copy of a wonderful book (they can't remember the artist or title) printed in England. It was a series of pictures of the life of Jesus with authentic Palestinian backgrounds, and had the scripture text opposite each picture. The list of resources in the back of this study book, the public library, and the nearest bookstore that handles Bible storybooks and other materials for children will help you to find suitable ones to use.

Another family had a big scrapbook, made by the teenagers of the church, containing many Bible verses. Each one was chosen because it could be illustrated with pictures of life today, cut from many magazines and other sources.

There are many selections from the scripture for children, excellently printed, sometimes with illustrations and sometimes with only the text. The use of such books in family worship saves much time for parents who often find it difficult to choose from the Bible itself the stories and passages that will be most meaningful to children.

There are Bible stories retold in modern language, with special attention given to the age of the child with whom the stories are to be used. In one family, when a story for five-year-old Marcia is to be used, it is Dick, the twelve-year-old, who is given the responsibility for reading it. He becomes not the child who is supposed to be enlightened by a reading chosen for a five-year-old, but the adult who is presenting the story to his little sister. And so he hears again, through his own lips, the age-old stories of the Bible in their simplest form, as well as having the more difficult stories read for his own edification from time to time.

Many families may bring up the matter of expense in securing such books, different versions of the Bible, and other resources. Everything children need is costly: food, clothing, recreation, and books. One of the services a church may well perform for its parents is to have a bookfair where the best books are exhibited. From this collection the parents may choose those books they wish to buy for gifts or for their use at home with their children.

A church may set up a Home-Use Library, with each parent contributing a set sum to start purchasing books which may be borrowed by the families. Here is a service in keeping the library functioning which will help bring richness to private devotions for the children, to family worship, to story hours, to times for browsing, to reading aloud at special times.

In these days when such rich and excellent material is sent home with the children, any parent can take from it Bible materials that have been carefully chosen. These may come from the Sunday church schools, vacation church schools, and other groups. This includes Bible stories, Bible passages, poems and verses using biblical themes, and Bible background stories. All of this may be put into a scrapbook for the future use and enrichment of the life of the family. One hour a week would build up a wonderful file of rich resources from the Bible for the members of the family. This hour may be a family project of inestimable worth.

- Make a list of ways in which the content of the Bible in one form or another should be entering into the lives of the children of your congregation.

What can you as one of a group of parents, by yourself as teacher or parent, or as one of the group of teachers, do to help a child to use the Bible whose family will not cooperate? What can you put into the child's hands that is so interesting, attractive, and worth while that he will want to use the Bible to the extent that you are making it possible?

This text cannot solve your problems for you. All it can do is to start you seeing the opportunities that wait for your ingenuity, concern, and devotion.

There is little, blind Jennie in the second grade. She lives at the school for the blind, but is brought for church school and is in your class. None of the aids for sighted children will help her in her "home." What can you do for her? What, for twelve-year-old Donald from the school for the deaf? He loves to attend Sunday church school with a devoted teacher who translates everything into sign language for him. What, for retarded eleven-year-old Bessie who likes books and toys enjoyed by five-year-olds? This section of the text is to motivate you to do something for someone who needs special help in learning to use the Bible.

3. *Pictures.* A Chinese proverb says, "A picture is worth a thousand words!" Yet, the use of pictures which illustrate Bible incidents or interpret truth is neglected, especially in the home. One would think that no artist but Hofmann (or perhaps Sallman) had ever painted, and that Hofmann's "Christ in the Temple" is the only suitable picture for a child. One new church educational building, erected at the cost of many thousands of dollars, had copies of that one picture and no other in every single room, from kindergarten to adult! One wonders what religious pictures were in the homes of the congregation! Yet, pictures are a lovely and important aid to Christian training.

Framing is expensive. It costs little more (or a clever person can fix it) to have the back of a frame removable. Uniform mounts can be used for many pictures that illustrate Bible incidents, teachings, attitudes, or incidents of Christian living. Sometimes a masterpiece is so lovely and its framing so appropriate that it needs to be left in the frame, but perhaps put away from time to time, to be returned to its place later with fresh interest.

One family celebrates Christmas by taking down all secular pictures and putting up the most beautiful pictures of the first Christmas that they have been able to collect. Some are framed. Some or merely mounted on wrapping paper and fastened with plastic adhesive to the wall. Each child has a choice.

One teen-ager was much taken with an old scene by Fra Angelica which had been painted above the door of a traveler's refuge kept by monks. It showed the weary pilgrim coming to the door and being welcomed tenderly. But Fra Angelica's pilgrim was faintly haloed. The unknowing monks were welcoming the Christ! This picture held out an ideal for the teen-age girl and she saw herself welcoming those coming for comfort or help to her home as she would welcome the Lord himself.

Pictures that hang on walls, that are in books, that are loved, looked at, enjoyed, and sometimes discussed in the home will make a lasting impression. A set of Bible pictures for primary children furnished one family with material for family worship. Each morning as Ted proudly set up the picture he had chosen for the day, his mother read the story from the Bible. Older children gain much from books which present Bible pictures by great artists with interpretations of their message.

●   What Bible pictures find a place in your home? Is this limited to "Praying Hands" and the "Head of Christ"?

What other pictures might be worthy of a place on your walls?

Which pictures from the denominational church school picture sets might be recommended to parents as worthy of being framed for a kindergarten child? A primary child? A junior boy or girl?

Try clipping, very carefully, from a paper or magazine the next Bible picture you see, mounting it on paper, and placing it where you can see it. Look at it each day. If you are a parent, take some picture from the materials brought home by your children and do the same. Help your boy or girl to relate the picture to some attitude or to recall the story he heard about it. Life can be enriched through very simple use of pictures.

List several ways in which you, or parents you know, can be encouraged to do this.

Other Elements in Worship

Prayer in worship at home and its forms and opportunities have been discussed. The Bible and its handling have been talked about. Pictures and what they do for the enrichment of the child's understanding and growth in feeling have been considered. Think of the use homes may make of music.

Little seven-year-old Hillis, who couldn't carry a tune, came rushing over to the neighbor whose family always enjoyed a Sunday afternoon hymn sing, and joined in with delight and enthusiasm. Singing is a lovely form of worship, joining words to music. Praise and thanksgiving, petition and consecration can be voiced in a way not often possible otherwise for a generation unskilled in formulating its feelings in public utterance. Happy is the family where singing is possible.

A modern mother learned to play the accordian. Many a delightful hour was spent at home, in camp, on trips, and at the church in using our heritage of Christian music. Her family not only became familiar with this music, but worshiped through its use.

Another family used recordings of hymns and sang with them. This is harder, for the group must accommodate, rather than the player accommodating! Some families sing in unison without an instrument. Some still have pianos. One family bought an electric organ and the young son is taking lessons just so they might have music in worship at home. Any instrument helps, even a ukulele!

Stories, other than Bible stories, also are invaluable. Stories printed in church magazines often are well worth clipping and keeping for future use. The quarterly materials for the children, whatever the form, also provide sources for materials. Much can be found for family devotions in devotional books for boys and girls.

Conversation and discussion are part of family devotions for, while this is not direct worship, it often is as vital to it as preparation, explanation, or any other part of the time of the devotions not spent actually in prayer to God.

- If you were counseling a family as to what they could do to begin for the first time the practice of worship in their home, what would you suggest? Make it practical. List and describe the members of the family. Suggest what will be easiest to carry out. What materials that are easily secured would you suggest? Remember that this imaginary family has never opened a Bible at home and wouldn't have an idea where to find a story in it.

Or take a church family known to have rich times of worship. What do you think you could take for granted that they would include in their provision for worship as individuals and a family group? What might a teacher plan to help a child in a family resistant to religion?

For your own worship times at home, list three kinds of improvement and enrichment that you could carry forward.

6.   *When Worship Is Spontaneous*

This chapter will be limited to thinking about times when a child worships naturally. Worship happens not because a situation or a place has been arranged, nor because this or that has been done, but because the child suddenly feels close to God. Perhaps it should be admitted here, with contrition, that in all too many cases, it seems that the utmost is done to discourage this spontaneous worship.

You probably know the story of Tommy who announced, "I told God I was sorry, and he said, 'It's quite all right, Tommy. I often make mistakes myself.'"

There is also the story of Janet who remarked, "God told me there's a lion outside in the street."

How many parents of a Tommy would be sympathetic and say something like, "I know, Tommy. God understands so well and is ready to forgive us when we are sorry. He gives us a comfortable feeling about it, doesn't he?"

If you cannot see beyond the imaginative statements of childhood to the truth of feeling, assurance, and consciousness of God as a loving friend, you will have difficulty in helping children seek and maintain closeness with God.

Janet's remark is different. The big dog she saw caused the idea to flash into her mind, "It's a lion!" and she attributed the information to God. Nevertheless, Janet also felt close to God and needed to be gently guided to more realistic ideas.

Young children with a Christian background in the home and with ability to reach out beyond their physical surroundings, often think and speak of and to God with simple assurance. This may continue until some embrarrassed adult lets them know that God is someone to be reserved for special times and seasons!

- At this point, look back to your own childhood and to things that children you know have said—anything that would give you reason to think that children have moments when no adult purpose or guidance is at hand; when they think about God and feel his nearness or the assurance of his concern. Do not be glib about this. Think seriously about remarks, expressions on small faces, and try to discover what was happening in the child's mind. Of course, you cannot be sure, but try to find a reasonably probable instance of a child's closeness to God.

A child is walking in the garden beside you. She is only three or four years old. She seemingly is busy looking at the flowers and the butterflies. Then, suddenly, a little hand is slipped into yours. Nothing is said; but in that gesture the child has said, "I know you are here. I love you. I want to touch you. I want you to help me. I just want to be sure you are close to me."

If what is said at the beginning of this text is true, that often is what constitutes one phase of worship for a young child, an older child, or an adult. In the midst of almost any experience that life holds, there comes a bright consciousness that God is right there! The mind reaches out to lay hold of the Eternal's hand and in that moment says, without putting it into words, "I know you are here. I love you. I want to touch you. I want you to stay close to me."

- In your own experience as a child, or as an adult, can you recall moments when you have had that sort of feeling about God and have spoken in love and adoration by being joyfully conscious of his presence?

Try to find a copy of some of the writings or the story of Brother Lawrence. Through constant practice of the presence of God he became what he was. You will find it worth while to read about him at this point in this study. One cannot, in all likelihood, become a Brother Lawrence, but anyone can practice the presence of God, beginning where he is now. Spontaneous worship, the bubbling up of joy in God, comes from a sense of God's nearness. It sometimes consists of joy, sometimes of comfort, sometimes of commitment, and sometimes of contrition. Often it is unspoken except in the heart. Sometimes it finds words or acts of expression.

Do not imagine that for an adult who has reserved God for Sunday, for times of emergency, or even for regular times of devotion, that the finding of him in all of life is immediate. "Seek" means just that. It means time and devotion given to a search. "You shall find" is in God's good time, not ours. But down through the ages and in our day, too many persons have had this deep sense of God's presence for its reality to be doubted.

Those who go hand in hand with God can more easily join children in spontaneous worship than can those who are diligently looking for something in a child's experience which they themselves do not know, even though they believe that it can exist.

Four-year-old Louise had an enchanting habit of composing and delivering long musical "songs," making up the words and music as she went along. This happened when she was alone or, occasionally, when someone she loved deeply was alone with her. It was possible, when the mood was right, to ask softly, "Would you like to sing one of your songs now, Louise?" She would nod vigorously, sit up straight with her hands in her lap, gaze into the distance, and begin. The "song" ranged into thoughts one would not expect of a four-year-old. Sometimes they were ballad-like, telling a story about imaginary people and what they thought, did, and said.

Louise was letting thoughts come to the surface and, as she uttered them, they became more solid, less nebulous. The music helped, too, for one can chant about that of which one cannot speak.

It would be easy to say that Louise sang about God. She didn't. Her home environment was not Christian, but she sang about everything else in her experience. The ability of young children to think about deep things should be used to let them utter their own thoughts. Watch for those with creative imagination and ability to put into singing what they are thinking.

● It was said earlier that this chapter is not about planned experiences that will eventuate in worship. But there is need to be alert so as to sense the times when a child who may be drawing a picture or playing house, begins to sing to himself, and the song is of God. You may or may not have known such a moment. What would you do if it occurred? There are moments so delicate that touching them causes them to cease. This is, perhaps, what one needs to remember most. Notice when and under what circumstances such moments occur.

When you are with young children, beware of filling the time too full of your own thoughts, the thoughts of others, or directed conservation and discussion. If thoughts of God came into Jimmy's mind while he was drawing a garden, what had you done earlier that stimulated him to think of God's being close to him? Take time to reread the paragraph which precedes this exercise and think about it in relation to any young children with whom you may have contact.

What does a person mean when he fails to be at church on Sunday and remarks that he can worship better in the out-of-doors? Is one inclined to think skeptically, if not to say to someone else, "I'd like to know how often he thought about God during the weekend on the beach."

Is it true, however, that most of the hours set apart for worship are filled with what one person called "chattering at God," instead of letting God have a chance to speak? Is it true that God might have a better chance to "speak to us in bird and flower"; that the heavens might better "declare the glory of God" in a silence that makes it more possible to hear God than in crowded times of worship? Far too often, from the moment the prelude starts until the postlude is ended, someone is speaking, singing, reading, or talking. All too often the emphasis is on "us" instead of on the worship of God, which is our response to him.

Think of that person who heads for mountain or beach right after office hours on Friday night and gets home late Sunday evening. Does he really feel the need to be close to God even though he does nothing to meet the need?

Is it possible that not only the youngest child, but that everyone needs spontaneous worship which is an unrehearsed and unplanned consciousness of God's presence and response to him? Is it possible that churches have failed, by and large, to recognize that need and make provision for it?

Why is the "retreat" becoming popular? Why is the quiet time at young people's conferences, when each seeks God in silence and alone, deeply appreciated by them? Why are some churches open for prayer, day and night, that persons may follow an impulse to go into familiar surroundings for a moment of communion and refreshment?

What is being done for primary and junior pupils in your church to nourish their desire for moments with God apart from times of regular worship?

● How have you helped juniors or primary children to be aware that God can be in every act of life? How have you helped them to know that there can be moments of awareness and a conscious turning to him, that make life rich with his presence? Discuss with others who are studying this text, or with your fellow workers with children, some ways of doing so.

The story of Brother Lawrence is a good one to use if you need that kind of introduction, but remember that spontaneous worship (remembering that we are God's and turning to him) is not easily achieved or maintained. It must become to us a treasure before we escape from habits of ignoring God most of the time. Think about it!

There are some practical ways to help a child turn his thought Godward from time to time. One way is with music. The chorus to "Gladly Lift We Hearts and Voices" (No. 49, *Hymns for Primary Worship*) ends, "Thou art with us everywhere." The melody is simple. This is one hymn that will come into a child's mind frequently, once it is learned. Use it as the children gather at a window to watch the snow fall; as a sudden summer storm finds the picnic party huddled in a park shelter; as hikers rest under a shady tree or lie on a rocky hilltop watching the clouds float across the sky. As you start to sing this hymn when the time is right, you will accustom them to use it themselves when they are in similar situations. Bible verses, responses set to music, hymn stanzas, and many other snatches of song will be used normally by children if they are accustomed to such use by adults. Parents can do more than anyone else, perhaps, because they are with the children in so many informal situations.

There also are memory sentences from the Bible and other sources. If these are to be useful to children, each must stand on its own. For young children, it is more important to learn, "God loves you," than "He cares for you." Who is "he"? "Cares" means two things: "keeps from harm" and "loves." Similarly, "God has made summer" is better to learn than "He has made summer." To the objection that this is tampering with the words of the Bible, one might say that he is having the children learn not Bible words, but Bible truth. Where truth is important, the exact wording of the Bible may be laid aside. Hymns are memorized, why not memorize Bible truths? There are many, many

Bible verses which, in their exact form or paraphrased for clarity, are suitable to help a child to flashes of acknowledgment of God's presence in his world. Such passages express praise, thanksgiving to him, or wonder about him, and also help to make habitual the child's turning to God.

- List from your quarterlies for the past year the verses, texts, or whatever the children are to memorize. Select those which might reasonably be expected to turn a child's thoughts toward God as they come into his mind, spontaneously, (1) when he wonders about some of God's creation; (2) when he feels contrite about something he has done; (3) when he is feeling lonely; (4) when he needs encouragement to do right; (5) when he wants to speak to God in comradeship, praise, thanksgiving, or commitment.

Have you learned and used the passages too? Can you lead the children, as individuals or a group, to use the right one when the suitable moment arrives? This is a search which can be shared with the group studying this text.

One teacher carried a little black notebook in her purse. With fine and careful writing, she copied the Bible verses that could be used with and by the children for many purposes whenever she found one in the church bulletins, in Bible reading, from devotional booklets, or from study materials for children. Once in a while she reviewed and recopied them, putting them into categories such as: Praise to God; Christian behavior; what Jesus said; Christian teachings from the Epistles. Her group of juniors became familiar with many of them in many ways. The idea in many of them, if not the exact wording, was ready to come to mind at any time or place.

One cannot be sure that a child will form the habit of feeling close to God or will respond in worship except under direct guidance. Few adults do. But this can be made possible, and children can be given the experience of doing so from time to time. Think this over carefully and begin to arm yourself and your children with words which may help to turn their thoughts toward God who is the center of all being, instead of letting thoughts remain with God's work which is on the edges of being, yet which too often is our sole concern.

Another form of spontaneous worship may come unexpectedly as the result of procedures which have been set up with no intention that they should lead to worship. It is at this point that some inexperienced teachers are weak. For example, Lucille's plans for the second grade called for discussion or conversation about homes, then for a story from the quarterly that showed how a boy learned the difference between a house and a home. This was to be followed by learning a hymn of worship.

The conversation was lively and, much to Lucille's surprise, brought out all the points that the story did. But she was inexperienced. She went ahead with her plan and told the story, which was an anticlimax and did not hold the children's attention. They knew right from the start what the boy in the story would discover. There was no time left for the hymn. Those children were ready for unplanned, spontaneous worship after their conversation, ready to express appreciation for God's plan for homes, and to thank him for their own and other person's homes.

Again and again, in the midst of conversation about almost anything, thoughts of God can become the climax if the adult is skilled in sensing the readiness of the children to turn in that direction. Lucille, who had a lovely voice, might have ended the conversation by singing the hymn that the children were to learn and, as an act of worship (not as a learning procedure), let them follow the words on the chart she had prepared. Spontaneous worship can occur in many forms!

"Let us all be very quiet and think about how great God must be who was able to create the world, the sun, and all the things of space," said Bill to his group of juniors who were lying out on a sandy Pacific beach under a glorious night sky. They had been identifying stars, and the talk had turned to how the universe came to be. They had agreed that it is God who created all things. Bill picked the very form in which those juniors would probably best worship at that moment—being silent and letting their thoughts wander and marvel at the greatness of God as they watched illimitable space stretching above them.

After a flower hunt, Priscilla suggested that the primary children make a litany, thanking God for the beauty of flowers and mentioning each flower with something about it that they felt was worthy of attention. The girls and boys worked hard making up their list, then tried it in the form of a litany. But this was not worship. Trixie got tired of what they were doing. "Why don't we just say thank you to God for all the flowers?" she demanded. "Would you like to?" asked Priscilla. The faces of the children relaxed as they nodded. They stopped work on the litany, and some of them prayed very simply.

Another teacher might have said, "We'll thank him just as soon as we get the litany done; you know it is a prayer of thanks." Priscilla realized that to drop work on the litany and have a quiet moment with God was far more important. The litany was used later, but it never achieved the sense of being in God's presence that the unplanned moment had.

Tony's class was saddened to hear that he had been badly hurt by an automobile on his way to the church and probably could not live. They talked about it for a few minutes, then wanted to pray. At first, they prayed for his restoration and for the doctors to have skillful hands. As they turned trustingly to God, someone prayed, "Dear God, you know whether he's too badly hurt to get well. If he just can't get well, then please comfort his mother and father." In the very act of turning to God their thoughts became more mature, and they faced death as being in the knowledge and purpose of God. They thought God's thoughts after him in their realization that the parents would sorely need comfort.

Worship is not always prayer. "God sure must have a lot of patterns in his head!" said Ronald, as a group pressed autumn leaves. They began to talk about fingerprints, how God has made persons different from each other in many ways, and how God must like differences to have made so many of them in the world! "Then we ought to like people who are different from us!" suggested Pauline. They sang, "The World Came to My Home One Day," as they went on pressing leaves. They were quiet after they sang, and their leaders felt that they were being conscious of the thought of the last line as applying to them.

> His Spirit, coming where we are,
> Binds hearts of every race.

- Recall a moment of spontaneous worship which came when you did not plan or expect it. Did you let it take over, swiftly and skillfully changing your plan so that

103

nothing might interfere with those precious moments of feeling close to God; the end toward which all Christian teaching aims? Are you alert to moods and quick to sense a time for silence, meditation, spoken prayer, or joyful praise, rather than finishing your carefully prepared procedures?

Spontaneous worship, especially for a group, is a fragile moment, easily broken or ruined; it is easy to pass by, unnoticed, the moment when it can occur. It is the still small voice in contrast to the tumultous noise of talking, working, moving, and being occupied. It is the heart when one is conscious only of feet, hands, eyes, and lips.

7.
Planning Worship for Different Age Groups

We are the victims of terminology: worship service; devotions; meditation; informal worship; spontaneous worship. These and other terms designate different things. The use of a term may result from the quality of the leader's preparation, the occasion, the place, or whether or not worship was intended.

This chapter includes all but the term "spontaneous worship," which is reserved for times and places when worship is not planned. The question is: How, when, and what to plan so that children may be led to worship? Perhaps some persons would like this chapter to go into what happens in the minds of children when they worship. Quite frankly, the writer of this text does not know, and has not questioned children to find out. "By the fruits" one can judge that the children have come close to God. In a group, a teacher often has a sense of group awareness of God, but for the most part, to attempt to tell what happens when children worship as individuals, is using the imagination! One may well keep in mind little Annie's pensive remark, "Sometimes I speak to the baby more sweeter than I feel."

What then is the responsibility of the one who is planning for the doors of worship to open to children?

In the Kindergarten

A kindergarten teacher without much experience took charge of the four- and five-year-olds in a new church which was being formed. She was without materials or a room of her own. She bought animal outlines for the children to color! They took these sheets home. The entire hour was secular. In too many kindergarten groups, God is left out. Four- and five-year-olds cannot worship if suddenly, out of a secular procedure, they are expected to think about and feel close to God. This kindergarten teacher was troubled by what she was failing to do. She began to think. The next week she wrote on the animal outlines, before she gave them to the children, GOD PLANNED FOR MANY KINDS OF ANIMALS. Unknowingly, she had planned for worship. With that simple line on the sheet, she found that she and the children could talk about the many animals God has put into the world. To her joy and surprise there was a happy delight in God's goodness and a readiness to say "Thank you" to God for all wonderful animals. She progressed swiftly beyond having the children color outlines! She grew able to plan how to lead into the moment of awareness, thankfulness, desire, or joyful thanks.

The kindergarten leader's plan is to make this hour with the children one in which they are at home with God, learning his ways, thinking about his goodness, singing and speaking to him. This is true in Sunday church school, vacation church school, weekday religious education classes, family camp, or any other place. Planning is based on the conviction of one's responsibility so far as worship is concerned.

A public school teacher and very successful kindergarten leader sighed. "The very hardest thing I had to do in transferring my skills to church work," she said, "was to learn when and how to lead to worship. It was too easy to say to myself that I was guiding the children to live in God's way, without planning how to lead them into God's presence."

How is this done?

1. Probably first in importance is for the teacher to grow into a deeper understanding and consciousness of the part that God plays in her life.

"I think God must be happy at the way you children played together today without quarreling," one mother remarked matter-of-factly to young Bruce.

He beamed. Then, quite seriously he added, "God doesn't like us to quarrel, does he?"

"No," said his mother, "I think God must be very unhappy when his children act in unpleasant ways."

Bruce was being helped to a consciousness of God's delight in those who act in his way. The emphasis was on what God delights in. But Bruce was quite able to reason out the reverse!

This was not a situation which would lead to worship. Any sensitive person could see that it was no time to attempt to lead Bruce to that. But was it surprising that Bruce prayed that night, "Dear God, help me to be happy when I play and never quarrel." Adults who are conscious of God's relationship to life can pass this understanding on to their children as opportunity offers. Planning and preparation is a mental discipline that makes it possible to see opportunities as they arise and, in group sessions, to plan for opportunities for comments and conversation that may then or later make worship possible.

2. Second in importance is familiarity with materials that may be used. A kindergarten teacher who knows Mason and Ohanian's *God's Wonderful World* (Random House, 1954), could well have stored away in memory the words and tune for "Thank You, God, for Snow." Unless the teacher is so prepared, the children may miss the joy of singing their thanks to God on the first snowy Sunday, with the added thought that God knows that children have fun in the snow. The prepared teacher will have materials which will help the children to choose what they like best about the snow that is part of God's plan for weather: pictures such as children in the snow, magnified snowflakes, birds on snowy branches, or the ground covered with protecting snow. She plans for enjoyment of pictures to lead into an expression of happiness in God's wonderful world. It may lead to prayer, or it may remain only a feeling. Familiarity with materials and gathering them with a keen sense of how they can be used when the time offers, is the result of planning. One cannot plan for worship by sitting down the evening before the group meets and snatching ideas from a quarterly or textbook! Planning is orienting part of one's life around the problem of what will help four- and five-year-old children respond to God's outreaching love.

Franklin D. Roosevelt had a large and valuable stamp collection. He worked fifteen minutes a day at it! Five minutes a day will enable you to collect materials, gain ideas and understandings which may develop into plans for guiding children into the heart of Christian heritage, the awareness of God's nearness, and opening doors so that children may respond to his love with love.

Worship is not the whole of the kindergarten program for children in the church, but unless it is the heart of it, the program will be secular. As one teacher put it, "Unless there is a *plus*, we have a public school and not a church school program." God cannot be tacked on. He has to live and move within the entire hour if he is to be there with any reality.

● Are you a parent of a four- or five-year-old? In what ways does your home seem different to a child who is from a secular home, a home unconcerned with or disbelieving in God?

Are you a group leader or a teacher of kindergarten children? Would a strange child coming into your group for just one hour notice any difference at all between what he finds with you and what he would find in any good child-care or public kindergarten group? How much difference? In what specific experiences? What did you consciously plan last week as an experience through which you could help the children to understand God better? Did you take for granted that because your group met at the church they would add God to the experience for themselves? Or did you guide them to see God as the heart of the experience through conversation, stories, pictures, singing, or whatever it was? Were you content to let God in for five minutes and then, with relief, go back to secular procedures? Secular procedures, in as much as they are life experiences, may lead to a recognition of God's part in life, but will do so only if you cause them to. You cannot expect a five-year-old suddenly to want to thank God, to rejoice with God, or to want his help if he has not been associated with the experiences of the hour.

Think about this. You may not agree with all that has been said, but it is a point of view which should not be neglected as you think of and plan for your work with young children. In addition, it might make your work become more meaningful and satisfying.

3. In the third place (although it is impossible to put these things in any real order of importance), think about the readiness of the kindergarten child for what some call "the encounter with God." It is nothing as formidable as that! "I never heard about God," said Timmy, confidingly. Yet his parents were members of the church!

"God can mend my dolly when it gets broken," asserted Karen. Her idea of God, as one heard this and similar remarks, seemed to verge on the magical help of a super repairman!

Polly was less vocal, but her face lighted up in praise and she joyfully responded to opportunities to praise or thank God. "God is our friend," she said positively one day.

Mark answered, "I guess we'd better tell God we're sorry we knocked over Mimi's blocks." No one else responded but, with his teacher's sheltering arm around him, Mark whispered his brief prayer and went happily back to play.

Timmy cannot open his heart to God until he becomes acquainted with him. Karen needs to widen her understanding of who God is, of how he is related to us and we to him. Polly is ready to sing "I think of God wherever I may be," although the thought is too mature for less-developed kindergarten children. Mark has a beginning understanding of the responsibilities God places on everyone for living in his way.

That is why that there is often individual worship in the kindergarten. The high moments of feeling God right there come in different ways to different children in different stages of development. Approach to worship is along different lines. Karen is ready to learn to say, "Thank you, God, for helpers who mend our clothes and our toys and fix things." A story? A conversation? A picture? There is something which will help her to know that God doesn't work magic but works through people. Timmy will rapidly absorb an atmosphere of love for God and join in happy praise, but his individual need is to know about the God whom he will come to love and to whom he will respond.

It is easy to advance "pretty ideas," instead of true ones. An old lady had treasured from childhood a rather fine print of Plockhorst's "Guardian Angel" in an old-fashioned but beautiful frame. She presented it to the Kindergarten Department. The picture is of two children playing on the edge of a frightful cliff, and an angel is keeping them safe. The superintendent hung it up for a week or so, high enough so that the children wouldn't notice it, and then found she needed seasonal material and had to store it. Why? That picture said to every child who might look at it, "It is perfectly safe to go and play in dangerous places where you are not allowed to go. God will send his angel to see that nothing happens to you."

The newspapers constantly report the deaths of children not because they go into dangerous places deliberately, but because they fall into hidden holes and innocently climb into old refrigerators. What is God's guardian angel doing at this point? Preparation for worship should not mislead children as to God's way of working.

This is not to say that God never turns danger aside from a child. It is saying that from the very beginning young children need to begin to understand that God has put us in a world of peril in which there are accidents, sorrow, and death. They need to learn to turn to him for courage and help in being obedient, in using their understanding to keep out of unsafe places, and to feel that in danger he is with them, loving them and concerned about them.

There is more to worship than planning a song that will follow a story, or a prayer that will come when the children have felt the wonder of God's world in sunset and birdsong at nightfall. Love, which is the foundation of worship, comes from knowing God as love. This is the foundation for the child's feeling for an adored person, and it comes from knowing that person. Compare the "thank you" for a birthday gift that Beth dictates to Aunt Mary who she has never seen to the "thank you" to her mother. You can convey to Beth as keen a sense of God's reality and nearness as you yourself feel. It will not be seeing, but it will be just as real. As she is provided with those things which help her to know more about God and to understand him and his will for a child's way of living, as she is given opportunity and encouragement to join in a direct approach to God, love blossoms even more fully into worship.

- Because work with kindergarten children is largely individual, think now of each child in your group, in your family, and your neighborhood if you have intimate contacts with them. What ideas does each child have about God? These may be revealed by remarks, reactions, attitudes, and comments as well as by any seeming relation of action to what "makes God happy." What degree of readiness does each seem to have for a warm, friendly, close feeling to God? Are there any who seem to have no feeling for God at all? Remember that one cannot know what a child is feeling "inside himself."

Does Susie pray most happily as one of a group? Is Josie learning to want to express herself to God? Does Richard find satisfaction only in the times that he finds out more about God's plans for his world and his people? Does Philip seemingly ignore completely any presence beyond what he can physically see and touch?

Think of various things you may plan to guide each child just a little further along the path of awareness of and love for God. Keep in mind, as you seek God's guidance for this delicate task, that a crocus opens in March but that chrysanthemums bloom in September.

As you guide four- and five-year-olds through planned experiences which may open their hearts to worship, your own experiences of God and your desire to respond to his outreaching love will be your greatest asset. Be ready with materials of worship which may lead to knowledge of God and love for him. In addition, keenly appreciate each child where he is now, and use considered judgement to lead him on from that point. This will make your planning an exciting venture. You will fail often. Everyone does. You will succeed often. You will grow as your children and your helpers grow more conscious of God's presence in all of life, and more able to sense his outreaching love.

In the Primary Department

Six-, seven-, and eight-year-olds, in most church-sponsored activities, can do things as a group in a way that kindergarten children cannot. One difference is that they can take part in what we sometimes call "formal worship."

Because this is true, many vacation church schools, day camps, Sunday church schools, weekday church schools, as well as other groups involving these children, have periods of planned worship. However, informal worship with these children can occur as often as in the group of preschool children.

Mrs. Smith always planned a worship service for her department. Very oddly, Mrs. Connor, Mrs. Lester, and Miss Adams, who each taught a class, seemed to feel that Mrs. Smith's activities ended any necessity for them to help the children in their classes to an awareness of God and a moment of closeness to him.

• Stop for a moment and find out how many in this leadership class, studying this text, are class teachers in primary or junior groups. Ask each to write on a slip of paper, unsigned, "Yes, I work toward moments of worship in my class procedures," or "No, I feel that worship is taken care of in the group program." You may be surprised.

All that has been said about the leaders of kindergarten children is also true of those who lead primary children; but there is something more. Children who attend school and are growing rapidly aware of the wideness of the world have a capacity for a rapidly growing understanding of God. They have a growing ability to realize their need of God and to welcome his concern for them. They can translate, from experiences of other children and from Bible stories and teachings, the nearness of God to human life. They can understand more about the way in which they can respond to him as they try to live life as God would have it lived. They can begin to prepare themselves to participate in worship, and deliberately quiet themselves to become aware of God's presence.

In addition to the procedures planned to make moments of worship possible, there are times called (for want of a better name) "formal worship." This, for primary children, does not put emphasis on "formal." It does mean that there is an orderliness to a time, not just a moment arising from circumstance, when there is deliberate preparation to set other thoughts and concerns aside and give corporate worship to God.

Worship does not occur readily at any age in unusual circumstance and under constantly changing form. Suppose you attended an adult service some Sunday morning and found that the sermon came first. Then all the hymns followed in a bunch, and the offering, the invocation, pastoral prayer, and the benediction were lumped together. In such a circumstance, would you be in a worshipful mood? If the spirit is not at rest and quiet, but is irritated, puzzled, resentful, or questioning, it is not free to enter into the presence of God for which purpose the worship service is attended. Familiarity with form is necessary in formal worship before there is freedom to ignore it and worship. As times of worship with primary children are planned, what, then, should be worked toward?

At a day camp for crippled children, activities were very wearing, but were greatly enjoyed. As each one finished what he was doing, he found his way to a shady place under a thickly leafed maple tree and took the sort of seating that fitted his condition. Some children stretched out on the grass, some had special chairs, some liked a big log with a backrest. A leader was there to welcome them and to see that they were comfortable and relaxed. They needed to rest. Quiet, lovely music played on a record player was listened to by some children. Others talked and laughed. When everyone had reached the spot, without any attempt to marshal the youngsters into uniform positions, the music stopped. They became instantly quiet and attentive. The leader began to sing, and the children sang with her. The words of "Blue Sky, Soft and Clear" had been changed to fit the summertime, because its delightful melody and words fitted that grassy slope where they sat, with blue sky overhead. They sang, "Father, We Thank Thee," and "Can a Little Child Like Me?" They loved singing, and each song spoke to them of God or let them speak to God. It was a lovely time of closeness to God in his world. There usually was a Bible story or one setting forth Christian teaching.

One day the leader said, "Do we have problems we need to talk about?" They did have! There had not been enough supplies to go around; they had to do an unusual amount of sharing; a child who was absent had caused a lot of trouble. In the light of the story and in the spirit in which they had been singing, they found some happy suggestions for trying to live closer to God's way.

Sandra volunteered, "When we have our prayer time, we could ask God to help us act the way we should."

The leader said, "Would you like to have our prayer time now instead of after our hymn as we usually do?" The group assented, and several children prayed. Then the hymn, "I Want to Be a Christian in My Heart," which the children loved, was sung. There was a sort of meditative quiet for a moment afterward as if the children were not eager to end their time of worship, but wanted to linger in the mood of it.

The leader asked, "Would you like to enjoy the blue sky and shade while George, Marie, and I get the fruit juice ready?"

That was formal worship. It had a form or design planned by the leader. The songs, the story, and the prayer she did not offer, were all carefully designed to make worship possible. Within the form there was fluidity. The leader knew how to keep the form elastic so that a conversation could be held if the time proved ripe for it. Sandra's suggestion was far more fruitful for real communion with God in prayer than if the leader had offered her own carefully prepared petition. Had the final song she had chosen not been suitable, she was prepared with materials in her mind and heart so that she could have changed it instantly.

Formal worship is orderliness, a routine which, with primary children, may be a bit fluid, a sequence of thought, and pertinence of all material planned to develop thought along a simple line.

• If you work with primary children in any environment, think back to the last worship with them and write down exactly what happened. Did it follow a reasonable order, thought out in advance, or did you think it up at the moment? Did it follow to a reasonable extent a routine familiar to the children? Was there alertness on your part to desert the routine to make worship more possible? Were there thought sequences in the materials selected and were these apparent, or made apparent, to the children? Did everything planned lift the children to moods and times when they could feel close to God?

Remember that when everyone else may have a high moment of awareness of God's presence, you may be thinking wildly about the oven you are not sure you shut off, and Russell may still be sulking because he could not have all the clay for the large project he had conceived. Persons are not caused to worship. You can only build up to the moment when the world can drop away and worship becomes possible.

For primary children this period of "formal" worship, or sequence of acts or worship, should not be very long. It is wiser to omit from these moments everything that can be put into a different time and mood. For instance, think of the day when plans are to be made for the Thanksgiving offering. This kind of planning is not part of worship. It is a business session of the group. This consideration of what the group wants to do may end with a moment of worship because it develops that way, but it comes at a time when the children are concentrating on whether to undertake something, how they will do it, and why they want to do it. Worship that day may be no more than a song of praise and a prayer. You may need to discipline yourself to determine the relation of what you are planning to use with the children. This discipline may be to decide whether a specific piece of material or an activity will be part of a process that leads to possible awareness of God and response to him, or whether it is something that will concentrate attention on other matters. Unless you do this, your planning is inadequate.

A picnic is an important event in a child's life. You may have games to work up appetites, or rest to quiet overly tired children before they eat. Each of these has a direct relationship to the picnic meal. You may decree a quiet time after the food has been eaten. You will not send the children in swimming just after a meal! If the swimming is the joyous high point of the picnic, it would be folly to precede it directly by food. Very well, then. If opening the heart to God is the joyous high point of the worship service, it is folly to put into the planned sequence something that will be dangerously likely to turn thoughts away from God rather than to shut out the world so that his presence may be felt.

- Go over a sequence of worship that you have planned for primary-age children and pick out what directly builds the experience as one likely to lead to what has been described as worship. Think back to the last time you interposed between the acts of worship considerations of behavior, planning for this and that, announcements about extraneous things, stopping to learn scripture or songs, or any other thing that failed to lead the thoughts in the direction of worship. What did these interpositions do to your group? Would they explain that on this morning or that, on this occasion or that, there was very little feeling of group devotion?

    This is something for you to think over and work with. This is not saying that these things should not be done with primary children. Announcements are needed. Plans must be made, but not when the time, the place, and the sequence of what is happening is supposed to be making worship possible.

The term "formal worship" has been used because it has form, and because it is planned in advance to follow certain lines. It also has been used because primary children are able to grow in moving toward a greater degree of self-discipline and dignity in their

119

moments of planned worship. But it is well to remember that stiffness must be avoided; that fluidity must be kept; that a certain amount of informality, provided this does not center the attention on the leader rather than on the worship, is desirable. It seems easy for children of this age to feel reverent when they are competently led not only by the adult who is standing before them, but by the attitude and participation in worship of every adult in the room.

In the Junior Department

The Junior Department is composed of fourth-, fifth- and sixth-grade children, no matter what the organizational pattern that brings them together. How does this age group differ, by and large, from the younger children as far as worship is concerned?

There are a good many advances. Juniors, especially the older ones, have a tremendous store of knowledge and can understand a great deal more than younger children. Symbolism has meaning for them. Their degree of self-discipline plays its part. They have abilities in leadership which have been developed in the public schools. They have had (or if they are only just entering into any relationships with church groups, may not have had) just that many more years of experience in worship. They are far more able to enter into group experiences with adults and to understand to a worthwhile degree the vocabulary and terminology of adults. In addition, they are facing a world of their own which is increasingly complicated, and are finding themselves with personal problems which they need help in facing, solving, or enduring. They have, by now, habits which will help or hinder worship.

Many other important facets of junior life could be mentioned.

This is important for planned worship for juniors because it is necessary to take into account their increased abilities, their maturing view of life, their deepening need of awareness of God in their lives, and their willingness to let him enter their affairs.

Planned worship for juniors needs to involve all the things that have been talked about as necessary for worship with younger children, and allow for two other vital considerations.

1. Planned worship must lead to conviction, commitment, loyalty, devotion, purposefulness, and feeling with God the needs of others. It also must lead to sacrifice, incisiveness about separating right from wrong, desire to act in harmony with God's will, contrition at failing to do so, and confidence in God's wisdom, justice, love, and forgiveness. These are, to some degree, paths to worship for younger children, but incidentally so as compared to juniors. Junior boys and girls are at a place where, if they are to bring much of themselves to moments of pure praise and adoration, they need to sharpen their responsibility as persons and bring their wills into conformity with God's will.

What happened, for instance, in a church service where a group of four young people had only recently graduated from high school? They had attended young people's conference and were seated at the front of the congregation ready to make reports. They whispered, laughed, and were so utterly conscious of each other that they had no mind for God nor for the need of those about them to worship in quietness and concentration of heart and mind. They were full of life! Life, for them, had not been related to the planned worship of God; or the planned worship of God seemed to them to have nothing to call them from continuing to enjoy life on a secular plane during the hour called the worship service.

The illustration of a group older than juniors makes more evident what may happen. It is so easy to say that juniors are restless, inattentive, and uncooperative because things are a bit above their heads. That excuse allows leaders to hide from their failure to provide the kind of worship that will be the roadway into the presence of God, and that will call the participants into consideration of God's ways.

2. Planned worship for juniors must take into account many more factors in its progress than worship for younger children. All that has been said up to this point about worship holds true. The high moment of worship is the awareness of the presence of God and response to him.

A worship service for juniors can have many moments of direct awareness of turning to God if it is properly prepared and properly conducted. Note the use of the term, "worship service," rather than "moments of worship." Juniors can give attention for a sustained period of time, as a rule, especially if the progression of worship follows the way the mind works in approaching God.

Some preconceived ideas need to be cleared away. A Junior Department leader was fond of having the juniors sing "Take Time to Be Holy," because she thought it had good ideas in it. She failed to realize that in it the juniors were giving advice to each other. Chuck was saying to Gail "Take time to be holy, Gail!" Andy was urging Sadie, "Speak often with your Lord, Sadie!" And so on. You are shocked? But weren't they?

122

If that hymn was being sung in sincerity, the fact that music was attached to the words changed not a whit the meaning and address of those words. The use of such items breaks a planned time of worship right in two. Juniors will not take that kind of advice from each other. Adults find it hard to take, too, so when they sing the hymn, they feel pious and do not pay much attention to the words. Perhaps some can transfer it as a message sung by themselves to themselves, but this is not likely to happen with juniors. So the boys and girls sing indifferently, their thoughts wander far from what their lips are uttering, and they are lost to the progress of worship.

Many other things can cause this to happen. One junior superintendent had the Doxology sung right after the offering. It did bring the juniors to their feet in a very familiar bit of singing after they had been getting somewhat out of hand during a lengthy taking of the offering. But was that the place for it? And was that a good thing to come between the offering and the prayer of dedication? Or was it mainly a mental "Let's stretch ten times before we go on, and get the wiggles out of us!" What should be fervent praise at a time for praise was being misused for thoughtless purposes.

Consider some standards set up for junior worship planned for group participation.

1. It must be purposeful; that is, it must move from one part to another for appropriate reasons.

2. It must be consistent; that is, extraneous matter should not be included.

3. It must be oriented; that is, it must be clear who is speaking and in whose behalf. The junior who is praying is doing so for the entire group. It is not a

personal prayer, and must take into account what everyone is wanting to say. If the ideas of someone else are being presented, that should be clear. "We shall listen, now, to what Jesus had to say to a group of people who gathered on a hillside to listen to him"; or, "Our story this morning has something to say to us about the problem we are considering this morning"; or, even "The writer of a hymn 'Take Time to Be Holy,' is speaking of ways of coming into God's presence during the hours of our days. Let us sing it, thinking of its being spoken to each one of us and trying to get help from it. Many of the ideas in this hymn could enrich our lives."

• Take some planned worship service from the denominational leader's guide which you use (or which is used in your church). Look at each item suggested. Number them. Then note: Spoken by the leader to the children; sung by all directly to God; sung to each other by all; and so on throughout the service. Look over the results. Is the orientation reasonable? Does it help the children to move forward, or is it distracting, interposing changes of front between the boys and girls and their continuance of worship?

Worship must be interesting. It must hold the attention. That means it must be true, beautiful, vivid, vital, thought-provoking, creating wonder, or anything which will lead the juniors to be better able to let God enter into their lives not only at this moment, but throughout their days.

• Mrs. Bond found that the time of offering was a point at which sustained attention on the part of the juniors simply vanished. After the offering, any mood, desire to worship, interest in what was being said, or concentration which had been good before had to be built up again. What would you do in a case like that? What part of the offering is worship?

At what points in your worship time with juniors are you losing the attention of one or more of them? An experienced public speaker is always aware of whether his audience is with him or not. He can and does keep constantly at work, bringing back into the group those who have mentally wandered.

Poor choice of materials may be your trouble; failure to connect the purposeful use of this and that; monotony of delivery (which does not mean that you are to tell jokes or suddenly shout, or do any of the things with which some religious leaders "hold" their people). Pick out your weak spots. Try to figure out why the juniors "walked away" from you.

Bored? Admit it if what you were saying was boring! Or if your material was badly prepared! Juniors are used to highly trained teachers in school. They appreciate careful preparation on your part.

5. Materials used in worship must be familiar. This means that even if, on some days, worship is cut to five minutes to give time to learn a new hymn thoroughly, you will so plan it. Worship time is not time for learning. However, this is no excuse whatever for using unworthy materials just because the children are familiar with them. They can and should learn what is worthy for the worship of God and begin to be able to use it.

- Is what your juniors are familiar with extensive enough for the worship they should be having? Are you having to substitute for materials suggested in your vacation church school text, camp guidance manual, weekday material, junior group studies, or your department worship just because "the juniors don't know that"? If materials are not familiar, work out some plan to make them so. Enrich; do not leave poverty stricken the materials through which and in which you aid juniors to worship.

6. Juniors may participate in leadership of worship. This statement may need qualification. Some adults feel that juniors should never lead in any part of worship because their inexperience and lack of knowledge distracts thoughts from worship to the inabilities of the person leading. This can be very true. To lead others in worship is a sacred responsibility. Yet when is a layman to learn to do so, if at each age, from childhood on, his "inexperience" is a preventive?

Probably the answer is that much of the experience of leading can be gained in practice sessions, alone with the adult who is guiding the juniors. Some things probably ought to be a prerequisite. A child who cannot read smoothly and intelligently should not be chosen to read the scripture. His stumbling will cause impatience, not attention to God's word. But even a poor reader may be trained to memorize a short verse and then read it well, and so take part in reading such as can be arranged, with several children giving different verses on the same theme—not reading one verse each around! When juniors can participate in leadership without diminishing the value and atmosphere for the worshiping group, such participation may be planned.

• Work out a tentative plan for beginning to train juniors to share effectively in leading a group in worship. They need to know how to introduce hymns, to read scripture, and to offer short prayers. If you are one who believes that juniors are too young for any individual participation in leadership, omit this exercise; but face squarely in your mind just when Melinda is to become able to lead the devotional in the women's fellowship, and Leonard to offer the prayer in the laymen's organization. Realizing this, you may wish to work toward group participation for such things as unison reading of hymns or scripture. Unison reading can be meaningful to a group if each feels the responsibility for making the reading a worthy act of worship.

7. Planned worship for juniors needs to be flexible to a certain extent, although not so much so as with younger children. It may be longer with juniors than with younger children. The leader must be watchful for the point of diminishing attention and be ready to do something at the moment—either to omit, shorten, revitalize, or even to close abruptly! However, no leader should consistently have to do any of these things. Worship must be planned to the ability of the specific group of juniors, and by and large should not have to be changed. Planned worship may be fairly short. (You have not forgotten spontaneous worship, which may result in times not set aside for worship.) "We need the whole hour for study," said one junior leader, "so we just don't have worship." What is study worth if direct approach to God is not part of the hour? With the more detailed planning for junior studies, many leaders find it very difficult to include spontaneous or planned moments of worship in the class period. It is all very well to study, but worship should not be omitted even if it is short.

8. Junior worship should be rich. It can touch upon the relationship of God to every aspect of life and help the juniors to seek God in praise and prayer, which is

related to all their experience. It can and should increasingly help them to grow into deeper knowledge of God and of his will for them as they worship in terms of that knowledge and that will, and to express commitment to his purpose.

9. More instructional material may be included for juniors to lead them to comprehensions or moods that will result in worship than probably is wise to use with younger children. Those planning junior worship need to be careful that material is not put in to "pad" the time allotted for a service of worship. If the story, talk, conversation, pictures, or whatever is used does not directly lead to some attitude or desire that opens the door to worship, it had better be brought in at some other time.

Planning for junior worship is a privilege and a responsibility. It takes everlasting care, thought, and openness to what is of worth. It takes constant spiritual growth in the person doing the planning to keep open the avenues to worship, so that they will lead to opportunities and desires on the part of the junior to respond to the presence of God.

When Ages Are Mixed

Just one word needs to be said here. It is that profound truths can be couched in very simple terms. These can be used in worship with a mixed age group and have meaning for all when they must meet together. However, it is essential that the materials chosen should not seem to exclude older children. "Can a little child like me," will be sung happily by younger primary children, but hardly by a sixth-grader. On the other hand, it is possible for older children to cooperate by joining in such a song if it is clearly understood that they are the adults and, in so doing, are helping the younger to worship in language they understand. Thus they join the ranks of leadership in worship. It is also easy to stand off from such a procedure.

In one church school where, for physical reasons, it was necessary for everyone from nursery to adult to meet together, even the adults refused to cooperate by singing songs through which the kindergarten children could worship. For adults to "watch" little children worship, or for juniors to feel themselves spectators at any point in worship is to "lose" them.

It is always true that quite young people can gain much from worship even though they do not always understand what is being said or sung. For a mixed group, then, it would be wise to aim at what will best suit and keep involved those who can understand what is said and done. For the youngest children, depend upon spontaneous worship or planned moments of worship within their session. You may agree. You may not agree. Be sure you have a good reason for feeling as you do.

8.
Worship in Many Places and at Many Times

Before considering this chapter, go back to the first two chapters and think again about the heart of worship and what worship is. In order to expand your idea of when and where children can worship, you will need to have these two discussions clearly in mind.

This chapter uses a different plan from some of the others. It will be far more worth while for you to think first and read afterwards than the other way around. It is too easy to read a list and say, "Of course! Of course!" It is harder to make up the list yourself, based on your experience with children and some imagination. When you have gone as far as you can, then read on, and be able to say, "I thought of more than the author has listed!" You will find it stimulating to "think of more than the author has listed." What is given here is not intended to be an exhaustive list.

One more thing before you start to work. You cannot put worship experiences into categories. That is, Allen may worship in an outdoor setting in a fir grove (place). His time of worship may be with his family (family camp) or during a day camp (special groups), and he may be a participant or a leader (conditions). So do not be too concerned with keeping lists exclusive. The purpose of thinking is to be more aware of the vast opportunities to enter consciously into God's presence, and to think less of worship as meaning "worship services."

● Think of the family members as they live together. Make a list of times and places when they, as a group or as individuals, may worship. Keep recalling what worship is—its many angles and facets. Do not confine yourself to one family.

When making your list, recall your own childhood; the visits to relatives or other families; families you have lived with or know as an adult. What is the scope of opportunity for saying, "God is; he is concerned about us; we think about him and respond to him in quietness and in all the ways which the worshipers find?"

Now use your imagination. In what other circumstances might some family, some child, or some parent worship? When your list is as complete as you can make it, read on. In your leadership class session (or if you are going through this study with just the members of your own department in the church school, or with a group of parents who are interested in knowing better how to help their children to come close to God), compare lists and talk about them and be stimulated to wider thinking.

Perhaps your list will be something like this:

Megan was looking at a beautiful Stellar's jay. Her mother began to sing and Megan joined in, "For every lovely thing . . . we give thanks to thee, O Lord."

Dad had been talking to Karl about some of the ways in which God has planned for the perpetuation of life.

131

They prayed that they might overcome any temptation to use their powers wrongly.

The whole family settled down to hear a Bible story that ten-year-old Clifford would enjoy, and then each prayed a short prayer.

On a trip east, the family stopped to visit a historic church. As Dad had suggested beforehand, they all sat quietly in a pew, heads bowed, and each prayed silently before leaving.

Doris had come home from vacation church school with a grace which the children had sung at refreshment time. The family decided it would adequately express their feeling to God so they learned and used it.

The family was to spend a month at the seashore. They talked it over and decided that on Sunday mornings they would attend the little village church four miles from their cottage. They discussed why it was the right thing to do. For several days before they went, they included in their prayers petitions to God to help them keep their resolve and to remember to tell prospective guests that Sunday mornings would find their family in church and church school.

Raymond went to Sunday church school, although sometimes he had to miss because his family was not interested and never went.

Howard's family attended worship services and church school regularly. They picked up a neighbor and his wife and children regularly, too, and took them with them.

When a church committee met in Sally's home, although she was playing in the next room, she noticed that they always began by asking God to be with them in their thinking and planning.

When the minister called, he always found the appropriate time to ask God's blessing on the family. Usually it happened when Harold and June were in for a moment. They felt good about it as he helped them to realize that one can be talking about almost anything and know that God is interested and is ready to help him to live as a member of a Christian family. They liked the way the minister spoke so cheerfully to God.

Bob was becoming an older teen. He often supervised his little brother and sister in their bedtime devotions.

The Towers family found many times of worship at a family camp, and they got ideas about how they could worship at home as a family.

Clyde cut a big slice from the newly frosted cake on the kitchen table before he remembered that his mother was having very special guests to tea. He couldn't think what to do. He prayed for help. Two ideas came to him. He put the slice carefully back in place. Then he went quickly to find his mother. She was annoyed but pleased that he had put the piece back. "I'll just put the cut piece on a plate ready to serve the first person, Clyde," she comforted him. "I'm so glad you told me, so I could have a plan worked out." Clyde went off to play, much relieved, and a quick "Dear God, I'm sure glad Mom's the way she is," flashed through his mind.

At a church picnic, everyone was silent for a grace spoken by the minister. At a family picnic in a crowded park, each member of the family had agreed to bow his head and say his own grace.

On a visit to Aunt Alice, Mother asked, "When do we have family worship, Alice? I want to let the children know, so they'll adjust to your time." Aunt Alice glanced at Uncle Henry. "We don't have it," he said, "but this is as good a time to start as any." They set a time.

Ted's little dog was run over. His mother prayed with him, "Dear God, we're feeling very sad about Whitey; but we are glad that she was such a happy little dog and that she died without even knowing she had been hit."

Don's family loved singing hymns on rainy evenings with the firelight glowing. Often, they found that there came a very special feeling that God was with them, and what had started as enjoying the hymn music became real worship.

Were you expecting this sort of list? Compare it with the one you made. Now, or at some later time, convert your list into one of life experiences! It is too easy to make a list such as at meals, at bedtime, together in church, at family worship, and other specific times. The best way in which to grow in ability to guide children in worship is to think how it happens in the lives of individuals and groups. Instead of saying lightly, "They have family grace at meals," it is better to think, "The Green family often sing together their thanks to God!" At times you may wonder, "Would this mean more to the church group at fellowship supper than to have someone offer a prayer?" Consider, "When does a person pray best—when he is voicing the prayer in song or words, or when he is listening to someone else pray?" There is a place for both, but for a child to really pray when someone else is speaking, depends largely on the ability of that person to guide the hearts of the listeners into a mood of participation. If you doubt that participation occurs inevitably when the pastor or anyone else prays, sit where you can see what is going on and, instead of praying, observe for a time or two!

As you think of times and places for prayer within family worship, you will find that guiding children in worship may involve your church in working with parents. They need to know how to plan family life to take advantage of many times and places for worship. You may have to guide the parents to feel the need for deliberately planning to use time, recognize opportunity, and create desire for God's presence in the affairs of family life.

A relative asked a young mother whose husband had no use for the church, "I suppose when you get settled in New York, you'll find a Sunday church school for the children. Or will Howard object?"

The young mother replied, thoughtfully, "I don't know that *I* want them to go to Sunday church school."

What she was saying was, "I don't know that I have any use for the church either."

If the relative had asked, "What ways are you planning to let God have a chance to come into the lives of your two little ones?" the answer might have been different.

Too often, we have equated worship (that is, becoming aware of the presence of God and responding to his outreaching love) with attending church or Sunday church school. We, too often, have emphasized "the worship service," rather than thinking of what does or does not happen there.

The family at the seashore, determining to attend church and Sunday church school during their vacation, were in reality supporting the church even though on vacation. They were being loyal to God and letting people know that they were Christians. They had a faith that mattered enough to them that they did this rather unusual thing in the hope of finding a time in which they could worship God. No one, making any such resolve, can be at all sure that what he finds inside the church doors will not begin and end with going through the form of worship, or fail to have any opening doors that might be conducive to moments of communion with God. If this family finds no true worship, what happens to their resolve?

As you think of times and places, then, it is necessary to go further and to determine that there shall be steps leading to moments of real worship if the experience is to become vital enough to create the desire for approaching God, letting his outreaching love touch one's heart.

● Now turn your thoughts to individuals. Imagine a fortunate child of the age with which you are most accustomed to work. Every avenue of Christian experience is open to her. This imaginary child, because of family, church influence, and natural inclination, has a happy relationship with God in worship. Write short paragraphs which you might call, "Clara Worships." Imagine Clara in all sorts of times, on many occasions, and in many places when she becomes conscious of God's presence and gives her attention to him. Perhaps this is for only a fleeting moment, or for longer periods of time.

Now think of a child you actually know and in your paragraphs check the experiences of true worship which this other child has.

Think of a child whom you know to be restricted in opportunity. With a red pencil, check experiences of worship to which you believe such a child might actually be limited. Be realistic. Remember those parents who attend an adult class in the church school in which class there is study but no worship, and who take their children home directly after church school. When are these parents worshiping? Under the guidance of such parents, what likelihood is there that the children will be led into the experience of feeling close to God? You are feeling lost and a bit discouraged at this point? What can we, as church workers or interested parents, do for such children?

After thinking, either alone or with a group, is there agreement on the following points?

1. Training in worship: that is, in understanding that God is seeking us and that we can become aware of him as we turn our thoughts away from the world about us and respond to his love; in becoming more able to relate all of life with its joys and problems to moments of awareness and communion. This comes mainly from two sources: a dedicated family, parent, or a relative closely in touch with the child in the home; or from church leaders in such groups as Sunday church school, weekday religious education classes, day camp, and vacation church school.

2. Extension of worship to all of life's moments: that is, developing the practice of turning to God often and informally as well as with others in stated times of worship. This is mainly accomplished in the family. However, it can be fostered through all church-sponsored activities, from class procedures to nature hikes.

3. Individual help for a child not in a family where there is a desire to worship: that is, where the church-appointed leader will be the only one to stimulate desire and to nurture ability to respond to God in all of life's moments. This is a responsibility that cannot be avoided and must be met with thoughtful planning and skillful guidance.

4. Help must be given parents to intelligently and effectively enrich the home experiences of worship. But why make everything so solemn? Worship is a joyful thing! And individual worship should be a delight!

Does your "Clara" wake up on a sunshiny morning with a happy "good morning!" to God? On a rainy day does she say rather pensively to God, "Well, I suppose the land does need some rain. I'll try to be happy indoors!" Or on a stormy, snowy morning, "God, I do think snow is most wonderful!"

Does your imaginary Clara have Bible storybooks geared to her age, so well written and so beautifully illustrated that she finds in them ideas about ways in which God would like her to act, and is she moved to think over with God what her problems are and what she should do? Does she have a copy of the Bible to cherish and gradually learn to use by marking passages suitable for her own age?

Is your Clara so familiar with hymns, songs, and prayers so beautiful and so apt that they come to her mind in moments that otherwise might lack communion with God? Is she able to voice her own thoughts to God? Are her own prayers in relation to many aspects of her life a joyous turning to God and a happy awareness of his presence?

Does your Clara have a deep feeling of God's will to goodness—that he is good and that he wants us to be good—and so is conscious of God's power to help her to overcome temptation: is she willing and ready to admit wrongdoing and ask forgiveness?

Such questions might go on and on. The times and the places when and where Clara turns to God would depend on her growing feeling that God is like the air we breathe, a part of life itself, a necessity to our very being, a source of joy, comfort, and strength in the life that God has given and has planned for us. To feel this, and to establish the practice of responding to God's outreaching presence is the basis of worship, no matter what the particular form of expression that Clara or anyone uses. Practice often will depend on adult suggestion, supervision, or leading.

● For many children, group worship in church-sponsored occasions is the only worship they know. Consider the following two statements from two church leaders; one, the superintendent of a Junior Department, and the other the superintendent of a Primary Department.

The Primary Department superintendent said, "We have a story hour during church and, just before we close, we have worship. In this way we can give our whole first hour to class procedures."

The Junior Department superintendent said, "We can't do more than cover the lesson in the church school hour. If the children want to worship, they can stay for church."

Think about these extreme examples which reflect too many situations and thought patterns existing in actual practice. This may be particularly true where trained personnel is not available to help persons think what it is they really are doing with such planning.

Think about your situation. How many primary children stay for a second hour or for church? How many go home? A leader who has little idea of the worth of worship, who so evidently thinks that class procedures are more important than communion with God, will not be a leader who fills those class procedures with moments of worship. What happens to the children who go home? A class period may have only secular procedures and ideas in it, unless the teacher or leader is keenly aware of the reality and presence of God. What kind of worship is it likely to be that occupies five minutes at the end of two busy hours when the whole group is listening with one ear for the sound of adult footsteps or the music of the closing hymn?

Think about the rich experiences that you would try to work into the procedures of that Primary Department if you were the leader.

"*If* the children want to worship," said that junior leader! Consider her. What do you think her own experience of worship likely is? How would she define worship? How much real thought has she given to the juniors who come from unchurched families and have no experience of worship? What concept of worship, as juniors can experience it, does she have? Do you think she would be likely to guide her teachers to find and plan for moments of worship during class procedures?

Both of these are negative situations. Sometimes, by taking a good look at barren ideas and the implications of certain failures, one has clearer understanding of the possibility of barren spots in his own plans. It also is wise to realize the implications of failure which can exist in the plans of even the most thoughtful planner. In this course you are thinking about how to guide children in worship. If you felt you were not in need of counsel, of comparison with what others are doing, of being urged to do some deep thinking, you would not be looking at the words you have just read.

These things have been considered before listing places and times of group worship that there may be a realization that group worship does or does not exist for a child in any situation, depending on the adults in charge. Whether the juniors plan their worship or it is adult planned, someone with an inner-radiant experience of the presence and reality of God must guide the planning or it is not likely to reach its goal. Skill is helpful, but how can someone guide toward a goal of true worship if he himself has never experienced it?

Here is the child. He worships with a group in day camp, in family camp as his family camps or vacations, with relatives and friends in churches strange to him, in familiar church surroundings, in weekday religious education classes, in vacation church school, in migrant camp situations, at many national mission points, in cottage prayer meetings held in his home. A good illustration may be found in the children of the Yakima Indian Christian Mission who lived in a mission dormitory while attending public school. They looked forward eagerly to the weekday evening when, if their school work was done, they were allowed to pile into the mission cars to go out on the reservation and join with older Indians in a prayer meeting in one of the homes. It was a real experience for them because, for the most part, their worship was with the white leadership of the mission, and now they were worshiping with their own people whose way of praying, attitudes, and background meant much to the children.

Must worship take place in every group or every time a group meets? To be specific, must that junior party have a devotional period? Common sense should determine the answer. Worship does not take place just because a leader makes a place for it. You cannot push a child into God's presence. Juniors on a wiener roast may plan for and welcome a time to say or sing a grace before the roasting starts or a song around the dying embers of the fire may work into a hymn of thanks or a moment of quiet meditation. On the other hand, a wiener roast in a crowded park, with many people coming and going, may not be the time when hearts can become quiet and thoughts lift to God. "Why do you try to have hymns sung?" a junior leader was asked. "We must witness to our faith!" she said sternly. There are other ways for the junior to witness to his faith—by words, acts, and attitude. Going through forms of worship, when he is rebelling at making a display of himself in public, is destroying his ability to worship rather than opening doors to God.

The leader must be wise and use common sense. There are a hundred good opportunities for moments of worship which are overlooked. "I wish you could have been with our first-grade children," said one teacher. They had taken a very small, decorated Christmas tree to a shut-in old lady. "They wanted to worship with her, and she added her prayer to theirs. I felt as if God were right there," she added wonderingly. She had led up to that experience as she told the children how the shut-in could not worship with other people, and how much it used to mean to her to join with others in singing praise to God, in praying to him. They had taken their hymnbook along so that she could read the words while they sang a hymn they knew by heart. They were in that receptive mood in which God can enter most easily into the consciousness of worshipers.

142

- In how many different places does your own particular group of children worship? Think carefully as you make a tentative list. If you are thinking of only your own child, include places in which he worships when he is with a group, as well as in your family or when alone. Think of the physical surroundings in these places such as the church sanctuary. Does the place itself help a child into the mood of worship? Does your breakfast table? Does happy expectancy, serenity, and a feeling that "there is time" make it possible for the family group to enter the mood of worship? Think of the junior camp. Are the mosquitoes so bad that the child's attention is centered on them; or is worship set for a time when few mosquitoes are around? Think about the many places where moments or regular times of worship occur and consider whether or not the physical conditions are the best that can be arranged.

It was very hot in the church school building. Outside, there was a little breeze. Wilda Jones picked up a roll of wrapping paper and led her second grade tiptoeing out of their room, out the door, and around to the west side of the building. She gave each child a piece of paper to sit on, for they were all dressed in summery garments, and she knew the mothers would not welcome grass stains. Traffic was going by, so she leaned her back against the stone and the children faced its dark cool-looking surface with nothing to divert their thoughts. They felt cooler, they quieted, and Wilda quickly adapted the moments of formal worship she had planned for that group to fit the no-piano, no-song-chart, no-offering-plate situation which now existed. She had them close their eyes and listen. How many sounds there were! What a wonderful gift is hearing! Wilda wove the distractions of sounds that were around about them into a cause for grateful thanks to God for powers of hearing. You, too, can adapt the unfamiliar to worship if you are one who finds evidence of God's goodness in all that surrounds you and your group.

Mrs. Baldwin was taking the kindergarten children to see the sanctuary of the church. It was not a beautiful place and an adult class was meeting there. But the organist, who had been asked to come and show the children the organ, had found out what some of their songs were. She set the sweetest, softest stops and gathered the boys and girls around her. She played some of their favorite songs and let them sing them, too. They loved it. Then she said, "I never play the organ without thinking about what lovely sounds God has put in the world, and I praise him for them." She began to play one of their songs of praise, and their beaming faces, as they sang, reflected their real sense of giving praise to God. As for the adult class, the teaching stopped. For them, too, it was a moment very close to God.

It was bedtime at a junior camp. Things had not gone well that day. No one in this tent had led in troublemaking, but all had followed a mischiefmaker. They talked over the day with their counselor, who was very casual about it and let them come to their own conclusions. There was silence. Then he said, "Are we ready for our prayer?" There was penitence in the prayers that night, and petition to God to help them do better. There, also, was gratitude for the place where they were, and appreciation for their leaders' help.

The organist used her understanding of God's gift of music and her love of children to make those few feet of space around the organ a place of worship. The young counselor had the wisdom to let bedtime conversation in the dark lead to the moment when the juniors themselves would be drawn to God.

A conference grounds included a lovely grove of fir trees. The young people had rolled in logs and set up a rough pulpit. They had erected a cross. It was a quiet place with streams of sunshine drifting down through openings in the trees. Children sometimes went there when no one was around, and somehow they became quiet as they passed under the simple archway which the young people had erected in an opening in the rhododendrons that almost enclosed the place. Sometimes they brought flowers. Sometimes they just sat on a log for a while, thinking, and then went quietly away. These were the children of workers around the conference grounds and they had been to worship services there with the older people. Because of the atmosphere of those services, the children found the grove a place of worship, even when no one was there.

A new church, just organized, was meeting in a square-dance center. Three adult classes and the whole church school for children met in the same big room. Tables, set on edge, made walls of a sort for the kindergarten group. Because the lead teacher and her helper kept their voices keyed low, they were able to use spontaneous singing and other materials for worship that are possible when children have a room of their own. The children were quite oblivious to the crowded conditions as they talked about God and felt close to him and sang and prayed.

Place is very closely tied to atmosphere, actions, reactions of adults using it, and mood. Yet, sometimes, all these fade into insignificance. A day coach on a train seemed to little Eric's mother just as good a place for him to say his bedtime prayer as any other. Made comfortable with cushions, and shut out from the rest of the passengers by his mother's loving face bending over him, those around could hear his clear childish voice as he prayed, "Bless Daddy, and I hope the cat at Grandma's has kittens."

Is this saying that any place and any time are suitable for a child to worship? Not in the least! That day coach would not be a good place to expect older children to voice prayer out loud or, usually, even to discuss matters of worship. No one can be embarrassed, feel conspicuous, and think of self, and at the same time forget self and the things of the world to center thoughts on God. If older children themselves seem to be unembarrassed or quite unselfconscious in talking about things religious, and if the adult who is with them can do the same, quiet worship may be possible. Often, children can plan a quiet time ahead, retire into silent personal meditation, and so have a real sense of God's presence in the most unusual circumstances. But remember that children are sensitive and you cannot push them into worship just any time.

God is ever present and ever reaching out to his children. There is no time and no place where children cannot respond to that outreaching love, provided it is possible for them to be still in heart and mind. There are many other times and places where it is not necessary to guide children toward worship. God has set responsibilities upon us, even as growing children, to work, learn, be kind, laugh, enjoy, and many others. The richest privilege which can be claimed for children is that they feel God in all of life and want to turn often to him, sometimes with a happy smile, with petition, and with praise because God is God and they are his children and are aware of him.

Two visitors to the Northwest were taken on a trip to the Columbia Gorge. At a spectacular lookout, the party got out of the car. One visitor exclaimed, "Oh! how utterly, utterly gorgeous!" The other was silent, gazing; but her hostess caught a murmur almost too soft to be heard, "O Lord, how manifold are thy works in all the earth!" Then she, too, began to exclaim at this and that.

Religion, said someone, can be caught but not taught. It would be more likely for children associated with the second visitor to "see God in the flash of a butterfly's wing," than for children who lived with the first visitor who did not then nor at any other time show any consciousness of the fact of God and his relationship to her or to his world.

9. *The Worshiping Community*

If worship is an individual experience, why should Christians gather together to worship God?

Some faiths do not. The writer of this text, as a child in India, watched from behind a pillar in a seemingly deserted temple in the jungle while a stalwart Brahman came into the dusty interior, approached the god symbol on the low, stone platform, dusted it off with a bunch of sacred *neem* leaves, and poured water on it from the small brass vessel he had brought with him. Then he folded his hands and prayed. A red mark was carefully put on his forehead to signify that he had done his morning *puja,* and then he went serenely home. Hindu worship consists, for the most part, of individual acts of worship.

Why is individual worship not enough? Why do Protestant Christians engage in corporate worship and become part of a worshiping community (worship in a group)?

• Before you continue reading, think about these questions. Find at least two good reasons for the practice of community worship which you could use to win an argument.

Part of the answer lies in our very nature. We human beings are gregarious creatures, and we get something from doing things together that we do not get from doing the same things alone.

Leslie came home very thrilled from a weekend outing for juniors. They had met in the mountain home of one of the church members. A large screened porch stretched across the front of the house from which there was a view of the Rockies with the setting sun behind them. There, just at sunset on Saturday evening, they had joined in a carefully planned vesper service. They had sung, "Day Is Dying in the West," "Hushed Was the Evening Hymn," and "Now the Day Is Over." The entire group was having a new experience of worship and felt very, very close to God.

Leslie was invited a month later for a weekend with the same family. Could Leslie, sitting on that porch alone at sunset, singing those same hymns, have had the same experience of worship or closeness to God that she felt in the group experience? No, she could not.

Could family worship on that same porch have given the same experience? That would depend, would it not, on the circumstances. The family, a worshiping community, might have a very intimate time of worship, but it would be different. It would still be a worshiping community, however. The worship that was experienced there by members of that community, including Leslie, would be something different from what Leslie would experience by going out onto the porch and worshiping alone, using the same hymns and prayers the group had used.

● Think of some experience of community worship which you have had, especially if children had been part of the group. Think back to the feelings that were present, the insights that opened up, the sense of community that was felt. First, imagine yourself and then a child whom you know, to be going through that same order of worship alone. What difference do you think there would be?

Remember that an order of worship in a community of other persons does not insure that a single one of the participants is worshiping. It is more likely, however, that a few or many of the participants are finding a closeness to God in the moments spent together in the various acts of worship. There are times when the whole group is swept into a high moment of communion.

A psychologist once said, "Act as if you like a person, and you are likely to come to like him." In a worshiping group, it is often true that assuming the mood and posture, the habiliments, so to speak, of community worship, does tend to attune one's inner being to worship. Children are sometimes helped by physical arrangements. Agreed-upon behavior, self-discipline to at least the outward appearance of reverence, may communicate the group's desire to feel God's nearness and to respond to him.

● What is your experience of the difference between a group turning to worship and an individual doing so? Think of ways in which group action and mood might carry someone into worship who, if alone, could not or would not try to enter into the experience?

Do the children in your group find their worshiping community mutually helpful? What benefits, what help in feeling close to God come to your group as they gather and worship together (that is, use the various aspects of worship which may result in real worship)?

Two two-year-olds were together for the first time. At first, they were shy of each other, then curious, then friendly. They sat in the driveway, tossing gravel in the air, pretending to be hurt, covering their faces with their hands and pretending to cry, then laughing uproariously! Over and over again, the individual but simultaneous play occurred. Even though it was an individual act for each, neither Sasha nor Patty would have had the same experience in doing it alone. They were reacting to each other's delight as well as to the fun of tossing pebbles and pretending to be hurt.

Five-year-old Titus was hurt when playing and he howled. His four-year-old sister Jane came with him to the house, howling as loudly as Titus. There is something about the makeup of human beings which makes persons feel with others. They are outraged and disturbed when someone is indifferent to the sufferings of another. Persons are called sadistic when they get pleasure from causing suffering to animals or other persons. A visitor from the United States who is *simpatico* is received with open arms by the Mexican people who keenly sense this feeling of togetherness on the part of strangers. Hostility or indifference greets the one who seems to have no openheartedness toward those among whom he has come.

In like manner, there can be additional values when the individual worships with a worshiping community. Attitudes, moods, and the feeling of reverence in the presence of God can be conveyed, just as can the delight of tossing pebbles or the sadness of being hurt. There is strength in community worship for it goes beyond the moment of adoration to common belief, action, and concern for one another in such a community.

There are some difficulties in being part of a worshiping community. To worship, one has to follow the procedure which the group is following. He may get lost along the way, particularly if the sequence is not wisely arranged. Some adults, as well as children, find it hard to pray when listening to another pray. The sentiment of a hymn, which is not suitable for a person to utter or not true for him at the moment, may be a stumbling block in his worship. However, when thoughtfully prepared, the community of worship is of inestimable value.

- What instances can you think of when children have had a heightened experience because it was in company with someone else? What worship experience might a child find is made richer by the participation of another child or an adult (such as having Mother present and taking part in bedtime prayers)? What part of community worship means more to you because there are others joining and worshiping with you? Is group worship with your children sometimes effective in bringing a child into that experience who might not otherwise find himself worshiping? Is there some part of group worship which finds you cold and not worshiping even though you are going through the process? Try to discover why this is so.

What, for children, is the worshiping community? Is there more than one?

First and foremost, the worshiping community to which each child belongs should be the family. Here the child is firmly established for bodily and mental needs. It also should be the source of contact for his spiritual needs. The feeling that comes from enjoying, doing, suffering, or needing things together should extend itself to spiritual matters in the family group. There has been consideration elsewhere in this text of the experiences which lead to worship, both individual and group, which can be fostered in the family. The worshiping family may, in some circumstances, be the only worshiping community the child knows. It is a vital community for every child.

However, no matter how much we wish it, this probably is not the basic worshiping community for most children. It is the church school. Statistics probably are not available, but one has only to stand outside the doors on a Sunday morning to see the children streaming away from the church building when the church school is over. For these children, the hour that they come to the church for study and fellowship may at times have no worship attached to it. Where this happens, they belong, no matter how faithfully they attend, to no worshiping community. This is putting it very strongly. You may deny that such can be. But think a moment. There may be no group worship in the kindergarten department (and in many this is so). Perhaps the teachers are not skilled in planning for informal worship, nor at sensing the moment for spontaneous worship. In such case, it is quite possible for a child to go home from this one contact, which might and should have been a worshiping community, with nothing more than that which a secular kindergarten would have given him. You may except the fact that some thoughts about God may have been given, or some ethical behavior in harmony with Christian teaching may have been encouraged. Just because a child "belongs" to the church school does not, of necessity, mean that he is part of a worshiping community. This need not be confined to children. In a certain city, a very popular Sunday church school class for adults draws dozens who come for that alone and do not attend church. The class is devoted to the brilliant teaching of

153

a fascinating teacher, but no worship of any sort occurs. It is a study group. Those adults belong to no worshiping community. Even if an opening prayer were given in that adult class, it still would not qualify as a worshiping community, for its members are there not to worship, but to be stimulated by an exciting teacher.

- Evaluate one group in the church school, limiting yourself, for the moment, to that part of the worshiping community and its effectiveness. Suppose a child attends only the one-hour kindergarten session in your church. Does it, in the right terms for his age, make his turning to God and responding to God's love a worshiping community for him? A worshiping community does other things than worship, but worship must be at the heart of its community life. How does the group you have chosen measure up?

  Is the experience of worship a child may have, because the leadership provides the opportunity for it, adequate for the individual for whom this is the only worshiping community? How readily does an unchurched child, coming into that fellowship, feel at home in turning to God? How soon can he, when he is alone, do as this new community of his does? Ask yourself other questions which occur to you as you think of the group you have chosen to evaluate.

Guidance cannot be given to help children enter into true moments of worship unless one knows to which other communities each child belongs. Janice's worshiping communities are (1) her home; (2) her church school hour with spontaneous, informal, and formal worship; (3) worship with adults; (4) as a family within the church family. Can a child, even a sixth-grader like Janice, be a real member of an adult worshiping community?

In a new little church, meeting in a home, the children were divided into two classes. The adults had one class. Bedrooms were used for classrooms. Everyone attended the worship service which followed. What had once been the living room was fitted with pews, which the children had helped paint the same soft grey as the walls. A friend had contributed a beautiful crimson velvet dossal curtain. Someone had made a simple pulpit, and there was a piano adequately played by one member. These five or six families, so earnest about their Christian faith, were willing to meet in such circumstances so that they could have a neighborhood church in a farming area where many unchurched families could not get into town. One man, to whom worship was very real, usually sat with eight small boys around him. They approximated his behavior. They sang with all their hearts. They could pray their own prayers in the "silent time," and joined in unison prayers and responses. Those boys, as well as the other children, were having an experience of worship that could not possibly have been theirs if they had been separated from the adults. When they had more adequate space, and when there were more trained leaders, something else had more meaning for them. But until that time came, and even after it became possible, the sense of "God with us," which that worshiping community had attained, extended itself to the children who were not just physically present but were a part of the community. In that particular instance it is only fair to say that the adults gained from having the children worship with them. It was an affair of families, and as families they approached their special hour of communion with God.

● In your church service, intended mainly for adults, what moments are there in which the children and adults

155

can have a heightened experience of being in the presence of God, which neither could have without the presence of the other? Think whether or not the adult community in its adult worship can be a worshiping community for children in part, at times, or in special instances.

Be fair in your evaluation. If you feel you must say concerning the solo, "Boring for the children," do so. Will the sermon help the children to a time of communion with God, to increased understanding of his will; or is it so adult that you must put down a negative answer? Will participating in the hymns bring a sense of response to God even though they are not too well understood? If the adult singing is real worship, this will likely be so. Is just being with adults as they worship so clearly worship that the children are caught up into the spirit of it?

So far, you have been thinking back. Next Sunday, sit where you can see at least two children. Note their outward reactions to every part of the adult service. As far as you can judge, what element has come into the lives of these two children because they were a part of the church group in its service of worship?

Have you considered that this and other times of community worship may be the only time that certain children are in a worshiping group? More children are likely to be brought to the church school hour and then taken home than come only to the church worship hour. Nevertheless, the adult church service may be the only worshiping community that some children know.

The at-homeness which the adult or the child feels in any such group is a factor in whether he will habitually worship with them. This transfer of feeling does not occur in a situation where the worshiper does not feel welcome, is not a part of the group, and has no sense of fellowship with them. Sasha and Patty would not have had a hilarious time if they had not come to feel friendly toward each other. A child or an adult can be as alone in a group as if he went into an unoccupied church. Being conscious of community of spirit within the group of which he has come to be a physical part is what makes him feel at home.

Harry and his parents visited friends in Mexico. On Sunday they attended the little Protestant Mexican church. They were conscious of welcoming glances. Someone pressed a Spanish hymnbook into Harry's hands. A boy his age grinned at him. His hostess whispered, "The Lord's Prayer," at one point and Harry found himself murmuring the English words and hardly noticing that the others were praying in Spanish. Since it was a small rural group, the pastor explained who the visitors were and spoke of them as brothers and sisters who had come "to their own home." Language and strange surroundings faded into insignificance. Harry and his parents, too, felt that they were indeed at home with these people; and in that confidence they found themselves worshiping with them.

For this reason, it is very desirable, when children attend adult services, for each child to be with his family. Thus they are a worshiping unit within the larger fellowship. One church has been careful to arrange to have "adopted parents" with whom children whose parents never come may sit. The adopted parents become for such children their worshiping unit within the larger fellowship. A mother who helplessly attempted and failed to make her fifth-grader behave in church was astonished to see him not only behaving, but entering into the spirit of real worship when one of the older men whom he admired suggested that the youngster sit with him. For that child, a worshiping unit of man and boy meant more than the association which kept reminding the youngster of resented, ineffective relationships with a widowed mother who did not know how to manage him.

A child needs close association within any adult group to become most effectively a part of it as a worshiping community. A child cannot be expected to identify himself with all phases of worship, but should find some in which he can truly find God.

●   Describe worshiping units within the community of worship which exist for various children who are present in adult church services. Be specific. Name children such as six-year-old Billy. His parents sing in the choir, and he always sits with Mr. and Mrs. Sturdevant who are especially careful to see that he is helped to follow the hymns and other sequences in the service. Or you may find some negative situations such as a strange child who is hardly noticed by Mr. and Mrs. Billman; yet she sits beside their Hildy during church. She tries to find the hymns but mostly reads her Sunday school paper. She and Hildy create a lot of disturbance for other worshipers.

Think of some other worshiping communities of which children may be a part. Remember that for some children any one of these may be the only time for participation in a group response, through worship, to God's outreaching love, concern, and presence. Some may be formal; others informal. Some may last for many weeks, or throughout months; others may be of brief duration. What are they? No matter what is listed here, you will be able to add to the list from what is happening in your community, or from your knowledge of other communities and situations. List them in terms of the children.

Betsy attends weekday religious education class.

Carol went to vacation church school.

Juanita found herself with a children's leader at migrant camp.

Tom went to Scout camp and his sister to Girl Scout camp.

Rosalie went with her parents to a Christmas carol service.

All the family attended when Gregory was baptized.

Buster was one of those at a children's World Day of Prayer service.

Grandmother and Grandfather always took Peter to old-fashioned midweek prayer meeting. There was no one with whom to leave him.

The twins attended church school and church the weekend they were at the beach.

Gordon and his family went to family camp.

Susan's family went with the Peace Corps to Bolivia.

Timothy's aunt married out of the Protestant faith. He was at the wedding in a situation quite foreign to him.

The worshiping community differs not only in composition, but in such basic things as belief, purpose of organization, and observances.

How can you know ways to make it more possible for Lora to enter into the experience of worship, as an individual or within a worshiping group, unless you are aware of what her exposures are? A negative experience in one group may constrain her freedom to worship in another.

It is difficult to know the background of every child. But it is not impossible for many worshiping communities to recognize the needs of children for opportunities to worship. It is not impossible to know under what circumstances and through what means they are helped or hindered to grow in ability to shut the world from their thoughts and to turn to God in deep awareness of him; to know that only as children can let go of the world, can they bring their world to God as they seek his help to live not only as Christian individuals, but as worthy members of the worshiping communities of which they find themselves a part.

10.   *Good, Better, or Best?*

All through this study it has been suggested again and again that choices be made from among the various hymns, scripture passages, stories, pictures, music, surroundings, resources, and other materials available.

There will be wide variation in what is being done and what is being used by those who will be studying this course. There also is wide variation in what is recommended by the denominational leaders who guide work among children. For these reasons, what is a starting point for some may be advanced procedure for others. What is acceptable or just exactly right for some may be regarded by others as too easy or too difficult or as entirely unsuitable.

Probably all would agree that no matter where they stand as they begin this study, they can move forward. To do so, standards are needed. Is the hymn which has been used poor or good? Is it good or "tops"? By what is it to be judged?

This chapter will have something to say about standards or yardsticks or ideas by which one may measure the resources used in worship with children. Not all that is said will apply to every worker. Not all will apply to every group. But perhaps all can be applied to help persons improve and to let them know just where they stand in what they are using.

1. Is what the material is saying (or causing the children to say or think) true? For example, many a poem, hymn, or song makes the statement that "flowers are blooming because it is Easter." That statement or thought simply is not true. In lands south of the equator flowers are dying at Eastertime because it is autumn there—not spring. The date of Easter varies over a period of weeks. In the greater part of the northern world flowers are not in bloom or are past bloom at Easter. Flowers do not bloom because it is Easter and the world of nature wishes to praise and adore the risen Christ. This simply is not true.

This is what is called a "pretty thought" or poetic license. Be sure to consider whether the poems, hymns, songs, stories, or pictures you use are giving the children truth or just a pretty thought.

Another example of "easy" teaching is in relation to prayer. A mother whose child had earnestly prayed for the recovery of a friend who was ill with an incurable disease, told her child when the little friend died, "Maybe we just didn't pray enough." She probably was thinking of the Bible verse, "Ask and it shall be given you," entirely forgetting that even to our Lord's agonized prayer in the garden it was not given him to escape the cross. This mother's statement was giving her child an untrue picture of God and his relationship to persons through prayer. It is true that we do not receive all that we pray for. God's universe operates on dependable laws. These are not subject to change at the prayer of the farmer for rain or of the children of the church school whose picnic might be spoiled by rain. Prayer is communion with God; not a bit of magic to secure what we want! Christians must be careful to choose hymns, to voice prayers, to select scripture which will be true to the faith, which is true to God himself and to his ways of working with mankind.

Another difficulty often faced is that of causing children to say, sing, or pronounce thoughts in complete variance with what is true about God and nature. A magnificent hymn has these two lines:

"His chariots of wrath the deep thunderclouds form,
And dark is his path on the wings of the storm."

This was written in a day when little known about God's laws of weather. When adults or children sing it, if they give any thought to the words at all, they are likely equating thunderstorms with God's anger! Truth does not lie in such lines and a congregation singing that hymn might do well to let the organ carry the tune while the singing fades away on those two lines. That should be done unless the individuals are willing to sing what they do not believe—or to put it very bluntly—what they think is not true. An old popular song, "I'll go where you want me to go, dear Lord," had to be sung with fingers crossed by most of those who did sing it. Perhaps they had no idea except that it was nice for the other person; that their plans for life were well laid without regard to the sentiment of dedication they were lustily voicing. It wasn't true for many persons singing it.

• Go through the hymnal or songbook you are using with the children. Have you the courage to mark X against what really isn't true? If the hymn is one that is otherwise up to standard, it may well be worthwhile to fit in other words at that point and make what is sung really true for the group using it. Do not be disturbed at the continual need for this process. Jesus himself took ideas from the Old Testament which God's people had to outgrow and said, "Of old it was said, . . . but . . . ," and he went on to give them what expressed a more advanced understanding of God and of his will and purpose for them and us.

2. Is the material you are using good? That is, is it good in the sense of being in accord with God's will as we know it? Does the beauty of goodness shine in the words, in the ideas, in the prayers uttered? Is goodness shown as having a quality that makes every child long for it?

This matter of goodness probably needs to be looked at from the other side—that is, adults need to assess their reasons for wanting children to be good. Too often, a passive refraining from naughtiness is required rather than a positive experience of goodness. Adults tend to admonish Julian not to disturb others at worship rather than to inspire him to enter into the goodness of worship.

But there is need to turn from this to what is good in a different sense. When is a hymn poor? When is it good in its format, its effect on the children, its literary quality, or its musical effectiveness?

In general, music should be simple, melodious, less prominent than the words and suited to their mood, leading to a feeling of worship if it has elements of goodness in it. Many musical numbers used in some places with children can, as a whole, be classed only as poor. We cannot rise to better things unless we are willing to take a careful look at the things we ourselves use or hear others use and admit that some of them are poor. Are children helped to worship when precious moments are used in singing a dozen verses of a song which include one stanza beginning "Zacchaeus was a little man"? The words are poor; they are claptrap verse. The song reiterates in a more or less humorous vein what is purportedly Bible information about certain characters of the Bible. The music is a good match to the worthlessness of the words.

If one wants to sing about a Bible character, compare "Hushed was the Evening Hymn" with its simple prayer at the close, that, like Samuel, one may have a mind "alert and quick" to hear God's word. Its music is magnificent and fits the thought.

- Look at the song you use most often with the children, or one that you sing quite often because "they like it." Is it really worthy? Does it help the child to feel the presence of God? Or does it just attract for other reasons and enlist the attention of all the children and a lusty participation because of its semi-secular nature? Perhaps you are quite free of this type of weak and worthless song. You may be using songs that are good in comparison, but go through this procedure. Are the words strong and full of faith and goodness? Or is there something better that is available to you? Don't be afraid. Children respond to the best. Two eight-year-olds came to their aunt with the request that the record being played be turned off and something more familiar be put on. She said, "You'll love this one when you come to know it. Will you try listening to it a few times? The composer is trying to help us imagine a lovely evening in springtime in a city street. The church bells ring, the people are happy, and the nightingale sings." The two eight-year-olds agreed. Several days later, their aunt came in from the garden to find the record player being played, and the music was the once-not-understood-or-enjoyed lovely composition that the girls had come to appreciate and choose as what they really wanted to listen to.

You cannot always start with the "great hymns of the church" for their thought is often far above the children's understanding and experience. If the children attend adult services, you may help them to learn to have some understanding of the meaning. But in the hymns and songs written for their own age group, and in words that are clear to them, you will find noble words set to noble music if you search for them. You can guide children toward these more adequate means of worship.

3. Is the material now being used rich in content? Poems, stories, hymns, and prayers can be like skim milk. Some of them are thin, weak, not very nourishing. Some are meager in message and expression. Too often, the same idea is repreated, with no enrichment in the presentation. "Worship" is the moving toward God, who is waiting for our fuller understanding.

> God is great and God is good,
> And we thank him for our food.

Often this is used with very young children as a table grace. But is it rich enough for the teen-ager, the junior, or even the primary-age child? Compare it with "We plough the fields and scatter," which goes far beyond the first simple statement in understanding God's relationship to our food. Why do we save this hymn for Thanksgiving Sunday when it is sung listlessly, because it is so unfamiliar to most children in most groups?

Many a child goes to bed with a "Dear God, bless . . ." for a prayer. Even for a young child this is better than nothing, although not as rich as it might be; but who would consider it rich enough for older children? There are many, many books of prayers which have come down through the ages as well as some "composed" by one person. From these one can gain ideas of the richness which is possible in the prayers to pray with children. Persons can learn to be rich in their prayers through such study. Children can be helped to know how to express themselves in their own private prayers to God in a way which they will not be able to do if the leaders' prayers amount to little more than skim milk.

4. Are you wise in your use of stories? Telling a Bible story in worship often is omitted because the "story" is to be used in the class session. Is the Bible so scanty in its stories? Is there no other story which would help to guide the thoughts of boys and girls along the same lines as the study for the day and yet be a completely different story? A story about Bible times, when it is made clear to the children that it is not a story from the Bible, often is forceful because it illuminates the times in which the Bible story took place. There are also stories of today which can be used. But here again, it is a question of choice.

When is a story poor? When it is poorly constructed. When it has no beginning, no middle, and no end. When it is just an incident, not a story. When it has no story appeal because of its not rising to a climax. When it is just plain uninteresting. When it is unrealistic. When the children have no background to understand it. When it has no message for them.

When is a story good? When it is well written with good construction. Even Bible stories need to be rewritten with great care, for often the Bible is interested in telling what happened and interlaces facts with teaching. For the child, the purpose of the moment may be to make him familiar with the story of an individual who faced a problem to be solved in a way pleasing to God's purpose, or who showed devotion to him, or determination to follow his commands. A story is good when it holds the attention of every child and leads each toward the purpose for which it was chosen.

There are many collections of stories. One way to learn a story for telling is to copy it. If it isn't worth copying, is it really worth telling? One children's worker had a loose-leaf notebook with stories she had found in all sorts of places. She had clipped, copied, and composed to make her collection. She was forever discarding those which were weak in one way or another for those which were richer, stronger, finer, more useful, and better written. Books go out of print very fast. A story from a library book may not be available five years from now. It may be a treasure you will want to keep for all your years of work. This same woman studied storytelling. She was able to take many a poor story and rework it into a good one with better construction, better arrangement of incidents leading to the climax, better implementation of the message it was to carry without being "preachy."

● List the stories you know well and can tell to your age group. Choose and study a story that does not seem to hold the attention of the children. Is it really a story or just an incident? Does it have narrative or plot value? Is it interesting? Does it have anything to add to the children's worship? Try rewriting a story. Should you make it more "human" by using language more like that used today, without resorting to slang or language so current that it has no beauty of form or thought? From a book of stories, pick the one you think most worth while from the point of view of content, construction, language, "feeling," and interest. Learn it and use it. Does it give you a feeling of satisfaction? How did the children react? Would you like to find a book on storytelling and learn more about how to tell stories, how to choose them, and how to rework them into better ones?

Everyone loves stories—from babies to adults. The art of storytelling is one that is well worth cultivating. Only as you work with it, can you grow in knowing how to grade any story as poor, fair, good, better, or best. This is a project that only a few teachers may take on without more help than a good book on storytelling. As they actually do the work suggested and learn to help one another, they strengthen their own abilities.

5. What is good in poetry? Hymns are poetry. There is exceedingly good poetry in curriculum materials, in church story papers, and in collections of devotional materials for children. There is also a lot of trash.

What guides are there for choosing the good in poetry? These are very specific. Form is the first thing to look at.

a) Good poetry for children reads as smoothly as prose, with never a word out of place to achieve rhyme or rhythm.

> "I into the garden went
>   To pick flowers firmly bent,"

is not poetry. "Into the garden" is misplaced in the sentence just so there may be a word to rhyme with "bent."

b) Good poetry does not place the emphasis on the wrong syllable of the word in order to maintain the meter or rhythm. "The flowers that bloom in the spring" has rhythm. "The garage that houses the car" does not. The first syllable of "garage" has to take the accent to achieve the rhythm—which means that the word is mispronounced.

c) Good poetry has a strong ending to each stanza, not just something to fill out rhyme and rhythm. "Jesus who died shall be satisfied" is an example from a hymn where a completely extraneous thought has been thrown in because the author evidently could not think of something that fitted the spot in that hymn.

The last stanza should be the strongest and say the most. It must "cap" the poem, not run away from the thought like a receding wave. The end should be like the crash with which the wave strikes the rock. After all, that is what you go to the shore for, not to watch the waves peter out as they recede!

d) Good poetry has something to say. Unless it can say it better and more forcefully, or with more meaning or more effect than prose, it might as well be skipped. Rich, forceful, short prose quotations may be more worshipful than poetry. Certain psalms, chanted, have a beauty that is beyond many hymns on the same theme. Some churches still use them. Others have never heard this use of prose set to music.

e) Poetry to be used in worship must have worship content. It may contain a quality that prepares the person for commitment, understanding, dedication in a way that prose might not do; or it may cause him to enter into meditation.

• Read the hymns you use with your children. Read first for meaning alone. Do they really say anything? Are they a clear and forceful expression that could not be done better in prose? Will the form of verse help the child to recall the thought? Is there beauty in it? Rate the poetry: poor, fair, good, fine, excellent.

Find a few poems which you think would enhance and enrich worship for your group. Begin collecting, evaluating, and classifying poems for use.

6. Is the prayer, hymn, scripture selection, prose, or poem understandable by the age group with which it is being used? Is its thought so expressed that children can grasp it and, at the same time, mature enough to cause them to grow? The poem or prayer containing the words "thy children, Lord, appear" is good for any group in which the members speak of themselves as children. It is good for adults who know they are all children of God. But it is not a good choice for high school boys and girls who resent being referred to as children and have not yet accustomed themselves to the religious terminology that, as adults, they will humbly accept in their relationship with God. The wonder of the word of God is that one perpetually finds its meaning richer and richer as one's experience grows. But, by and large, materials used in worship must be related to the understanding and experience of the boys or girls with whom they are used. The use of symbolism with primary children creates a physical image which may forever block out the spiritual meaning of what the words of a hymn, poem, scripture passage, story, or prose selection has to say. As a rather extreme example, take the case of the line "Here I raise mine Ebenezer," which is a loose quote from the Bible (1 Sam. 7:12)

that is found in one hymn still sometimes used. Not knowing what an Ebenezer could be, one child thought it likely meant the rear of his anatomy being raised from the seat as everyone rose to sing! Although understanding came later, the original thought still comes into the mind of that person with such amusement that the hymn never will be worshipful for him—never!

7. There are many other criteria for choice. As you begin to think about what you are choosing, you will find that often, with deep reluctance, you will discard even what is good, beautiful, and true because it is shopworn. One church is discovering that it is going to have to find Christmas carols that are not blared out in store and street loudspeakers, over radio, and on crooner's recordings if there is to be real meaning in Christmastime worship. You will find yourself setting up standards which will make worship evermore a true response to God's calling. You will become conscious of time lost when children lose interest and attention, and you will be ready to search out the cause. You will have moments of regret that you took an easy path in making choices instead of measuring your choices against the standards of which you have become aware.

It is the rewarding part of making choices that must be stressed. There is delight in finding the perfect carol for Easter that had never been heard nor printed before. There is the sober thrill of finding a prayer so aptly phrased, so rich, so fit to guide children's thoughts toward God. There is the amazement of realizing that in this story of the Bible there is help for problems your very own children are facing. When this happens, it gives evidence that your reading has been guided of God toward its finding, and that his help will be yours as you ponder its teaching and adapt its wording for use with your boys and girls. This is how rewarding your choices may be!

To love the best, to help others to love it, and to find worship more and more necessary for fullness of life is part of Christian growth. This is true not only for the adult leader, but for the children who are dependent on his choices for their growth and enrichment.

A resource may be some person, place, or a bit of material to which you can turn to enrich an experience beyond the usual basic church-supplied materials and personnel with which you work.

As you come to the end of this text, think about the boys and girls with whom you have contact. Think also about how you may begin to guide or work at guiding them more friutfully into experiences which encourage children to worship.

If you are an old hand at this, you perhaps know many of the resources upon which you can depend. If you are new to the privilege and task, a delightful experience awaits as you begin to build up your files and discover how much there is to help you in what is a rewarding, though difficult, responsibility.

Resource Persons

Too often, materials are thought of as resources. Persons are vital for worship because the feeling of being in the presence of God is frequently caught from other human beings rather than from using material, important as the right choice of material is.

Who, then, are resource persons for worship? Many leaders find it helpful to visit children's groups where worship has the qualities they wish to have with their own group. It is helpful to visit another group with the idea of learning how best to lead the children to worship, even though you may come away disappointed. Often, in such a situation, one can see the mistakes he is making much more easily than when he is in command. One teacher saw so clearly what a disorderly room did to the children that she was shocked into realizing that the disorder of her own department room needed attention!

Another teacher found children offering short prayers with deep sincerity. "I didn't know they could do that," she murmured. Later that week she had a conference with the hostess leader and found in her a resource for her own further development.

For the leaders of an expanded session with juniors, the whole adult body of the church became resource persons as the boys and girls came into the adult service from time to time, there to find worship such as they were failing to achieve in spirit in their own group. They were helped by these resource persons, many of whom were not at all conscious of having done so.

A group of primary teachers were not familiar with the right use of stories in worship. They asked a woman from another church who was skilled in this to assume leadership in their department for a while. As she worked with the children, using her knowledge and skill to guide them into worship, the superintendent and teachers became better able to see how this could be done. They also saw other ways in which they could be more competent in the leadership of worship for their children. She was resource for them.

Teachers of leadership training courses, laboratory schools, institutes, and many other training activities are resources.

Then there are the specialists. There is the man who is making a hobby of Christmas music. He can contribute richly to the group wanting a change from the music that is being blared from every store in town to something that will be more meaningful because it is not so associated with shopping and secular things. He is a resource. The young wife who participated in dramatics in school and can so easily help drama to have meaning and atmosphere is a treasure of resource. So is the music teacher who is willing to take the responsibility of helping to develop Arlinda's ability to play hymns so that she may occasionally help in the leadership of music, and later become one of the accomplished pianists in the church.

This is to say that any person, child or adult, who helps you gain something for yourself or for your group, is a resource person. Yet, how few of us search for such persons and use their help!

● Where are you seeking help? From other groups? From which individuals? From training opportunities beyond this class you are now attending?

As a class, list opportunities that each might take advantage of during this next year. Can you become resource persons for each other?

The Scriptures

The Bible is a resource. It is a special resource because it is God's word to his people. Remember, not all of it is designed for use in worship. Most of it is written for adults and not for children. Use of it has to be skillful and under the guidance of God.

You can be rich or poor in your use of the Bible. Become familiar with the forms in which biblical material is available.

A church school in a beginning church where all, from kindergarten to adults, had to meet in one big room, occasionally had a time together when they thought about some one special thing. One year they had a Bible Sunday. From their personal Bibles, visitors read a certain passage in Danish, in Lonkundu (the language of one of that church's missions in Congo), and in English. It was the first time that many of the children had heard God's word in a tongue strange to them. But the reverence with which it was read, the delight in the faces of those reading, and the introduction and concluding words of the one presiding helped everyone present to a new sense of thankfulness for those who are making it possible for the world's people to know God.

In a certain Sunday church school class there are some children from a nearby school for the blind. They bring their Braille Bibles (or parts of them) with them and share in the reading. The members of that class have a growing realization of how God can speak to them through the ministry of those who cannot see. God's word through the finger tips! There is a deep sense of thanksgiving that God has made it possible for the blind to hear his voice through the Bible.

Bibles and biblical material in many languages are resources. Juniors love collections. A Junior Department may well rejoice in a really worthwhile biblical collection and work to add to it. This may include large and small Bibles, portions, Bibles that crossed the ocean, or crossed the prairie in a covered wagon, Bibles that beloved missionaries have worn threadbare. A feeling of reverence is deepened as juniors see the wonderful illuminated pages of the scriptures such as the monks prepared. Sometimes these appear in color in magazines. Christmas and Easter annuals often have beautifully illuminated scripture passages. Christmas and Easter cards may be exquisitely beautiful with illuminated texts.

Gathering biblical resource is an all-year-round job. You cannot rush to a pile of magazines and expect to find therein a scripture passage or an illuminated text. The day before you want to use it is too late to look for a story about the reverence in which the Bible was held by a group of people in the Middle Ages.

Gathering Bibles in other languages or from pioneer days requires a mind alert to possibilities. Often a family is indifferent to the beloved possessions of a grandmother who has just died. A friend could easily secure for the church the well-worn Bible that is dated a year that will seem so far back to the children! Auction sales, old-book stores, visiting missionaries—all are sources from which biblical material can be secured.

Children's work such as worship posters, containing Bible verses or psalms, are often worth while and are a resource. This also may be true of scrapbooks made with present-day illustrations of the meaning of Christian teaching. Occasionally, something of such worth is done that it can become a resource to be used over and over again as effectually as something you find elsewhere.

Do not forget Bible storybooks for all ages. You will need to go over these carefully before purchasing them. Be sure that the story is true to the facts. A piece of material tells the story of Jacob as if he were a young lad going to visit his uncle. He was afraid when he was delayed in the wilderness and didn't make the trip as fast as he thought he could. This is not true to the story of Jacob, a grown man who had cheated his old father into giving him the blessing of the firstborn son and who was fleeing from the just anger of his brother.

Pictures in storybooks need to be scanned too. For most persons it is easier to rely on the screening done by denominational children's workers and to purchase from lists of acceptable books which they supply.

Do not neglect books about the Bible, the use of the Bible, and what the Bible has meant to others.

Do not fail to build up a file from current story papers, children's church school materials, teacher's church school quarterlies, vacation school texts, or other sources of the Bible stories retold for your age group. Stories about the Bible and its use also are often found in these sources. Take time to clip such stories or make note of their source and file them in loose-leaf notebooks or file folders. Such a resource will be invaluable.

Do not neglect biblical pictures, films, and filmstrips. You are aware of how these can be used occasionally to open doors for worship. Keep in mind that often the use of them is instructional and is *not* for worship, although instruction may lead to worship.

- What Bible storybooks have you for use with your four- and five-year-olds? How do you use these books?

How many Bible stories for this age group do you know by heart so that you can use them when the time is ripe? What Bible stories are you and your church recommending for the parents of these children to have in the homes?

If you do not already have one, supply yourself with a notebook. Choose two stories from the materials you have used this past year, which you will be sure to want to use again, and clip or copy them into your notebook. Begin to learn them.

Locate a very interesting old Bible that you could use with the children to help them to realize how others have treasured the Bible. Consider how your use of it with them might lead to a moment of worship.

If you work with primary or junior children, follow the same procedure with materials suited to them.

Could you combine the use of a person who is a resource with the materials which you will use? Outline a plan for gathering biblical resource of all kinds, including persons, which you might carry out individually, with other teachers, or with your group of children. Is there a parent who would undertake the care of such a collection, supervising anything the children need to do to establish it?

Music

The hymnal or songbook recommended by your denominational leaders is a resource for worship, but you probably will want to use additional resources. For instance, a book for primary worship may fail to include any hymns of direct praise to God. These must be sought in other books. Another book may include a most excellent and useful collection of worship materials as well as some very poor music and words that give wrong bases for later Christian growth.

What is a practical plan? One kindergarten leader has a loose-leaf notebook. Whenever possible, she gets two copies of collections of songs for children of that age, particularly anything put out by her own church. From these she clips songs! Into her own private loose-leaf songbook go the songs that she herself finds most useful for moments of worship and other purposes. There are tests through which she passes them. An unworthy song, no matter how beloved by some helper in a long-passed childhood, or how beloved by the children, if it has undesirable ideas or half-truths, is not included in that book. She often clips a song from current church school, vacation church school, or weekday school materials; from carol books, from any source.

One teacher keeps in her loose-leaf music book that which the children know. She works with the other material in her own way, getting to know it, thinking of where it might be useful. When it is to be used with the children, she transfers it to her loose-leaf book.

Other teachers prefer to keep books intact. But some arrangement must be made for songs and music clipped from quarterlies and other sources. The more methodical the arrangement, the more useful a resource will be.

A person may be a music resource. One department has two persons working in unusual harmony. The one who is the lead teacher cannot carry a tune. A helper can. It is interesting to see how, without a word, just because the two have a common purpose, the helper starts a song at the point where the lead teacher would have done so. They do some planning together, of course; but often there is an opening for something not planned. Sometimes the lead teacher says, "Would you like to sing . . .?" Then, led by the helper, they do. There is no sense of division. That helper is the lead teacher's singing voice!

- If you work with four- and five-year-olds, list the words and music through which the children, as individuals, enter into or become especially conscious of God's presence. Remember that this does not imply other music is not worth while; only that it may not lead to worship. Are you content with what you have listed?

 As a study group, enrich your list from each other's lists. In the weeks ahead go over all your materials and find other songs to use in worship. Do a little telephoning. You can note the words and learn the tune over the telephone!

 Check all the materials for truth, beauty, and suitability for your children.

 Is there a mother who is musically inclined who would enjoy helping you find and learn new worship songs for use by the children?

Hymns for use with primary children in worship are wider in scope. There are several collections of hymns and songs for children of this age. Many songs appear in their take-home materials and in the teacher's quarterlies and texts. Public school music books often offer some worship materials included for their literary and musical quality. At this point, you probably will need to do even more "sorting out" than for the kindergarten if you wish to use miscellaneous resources, or even if you are using your own denominational hymnal for primary children. One committee working on a new hymnal for primary children, decided to include a mediocre hymn at one point because they could not find words and music on that particular theme that were any better; but other hymnals have been printed since. Individual hymns have appeared in periodical materials. The alert primary leader will be able to substitute something far richer, more meaningful, and full of beauty.

- For what will you search to use in worship with primary children? List hymns of direct praise and thanksgiving to God. List prayer hymns and responses, calls to worship, hymns of dedication and devotion that you use. Divide into categories the hymns your children know. Compare this with the different types of worship music you will need. Now, as a group, compare your lists. Each may enrich the other. Set up standards for selection.

  Arrange a musical evening next month, each of you bringing to the meeting place that hymn or song through which your primary children have seemed to enter into real worship. If such an evening results in sharing experiences you have had and adds two songs rich in meaning for your group, you will have put in a worthwhile few hours. Research need not be a lonely business.

  Go to the library or ask the librarian to help you find what is available in the way of music if you cannot find other sources.

If anything, junior leaders are supplied with an overabundance of material. Yet, many of them use the same old standbys long after they cease to mean anything to the children. One junior superintendent inspired her Junior Department to learn every single hymn and response in their hymnal! They decided they wanted to be able to sing whatever they needed, when they needed it, without stopping to learn it! That leader brought the entire resource of the junior hymnal to life in her children's hearts and minds. She did more than that. She made them see the delight of learning new things.

Another junior superintendent decided that some new Christmas carols would be helpful. She asked the juniors to study the words of all that she had collected and choose which they would like. The boys and girls surprised her by choosing some of real worth. That leader was exposing her pupils to resources from which they enjoyed choosing and which helped them to want to learn new things. In both cases the leader had a vision of reaching out beyond the usual and making use of resource.

For juniors, the adult hymnal has many possibilities. When juniors are in the adult service of worship, it is desirable that they have help in understanding, so far as they can, the meaning of what they are to sing.

There are junior choir books as well as youth and other hymnals, carol books, public school music which contains hymns, and camp songbooks.

Resource is everywhere. Gather it together. Pick out the very best. Test it with the children. List your needs for the various phases of worship and note what resources you list under each. Keep on collecting music, then cull from it the best.

- Compare the book you are using with your juniors with the books that other members of this study group are using. Would a copy of one other book help you?

  What six hymns of praise to God do your juniors know so that you can alternate them? What responses of thanksgiving do they know? What hymns of pure praise and responses of thanksgiving are among your resources which you could teach them?

If you do not have adequate worship material, work out a plan to secure some. One junior superintendent, who always had used for her department the hymnals discarded by the adults, felt the need of more suitable resource. The junior hymnal she wanted cost a dollar and a half. The church school budget did not include money for a junior hymnal, and the superintendent was not able to spare that money. Or was she? She decided she could set aside ten cents a week. Four months later she had her hymnal, and with words lettered on wrapping paper she was able to bring a new quality to worship to her boys and girls. Sometimes resource costs. What would you like to have? How can you get it? Many teachers find church boards eager to spend money for things really needed for the children.

Pictures

There is no resource quite like pictures! They are far easier to find now than they were twenty-five years ago. Yet, even as their worth is recognized, it must also be admitted that there are very few pictures which of themselves actually lead into worship. There are a few.

An abstract painting, glorious in golden light and shimmering movement, painted by a man who seemingly has no belief in God, brings one to a breathless standstill with the words, "And God said, 'Let there be light!'" echoing in one's mind. Pictures which carry one's thoughts to God are resource for worship.

There are more pictures for use in the moments of story, conversation, and information which lead forward to worship. There are those that bring to mind that for which one is thankful. These need not be described in detail. Each teacher should have an ample supply of this type of pictures.

There are pictures which help to set the mood for worship. For instance, children may come into a room when thanksgiving to God for the beauties of his world is going to be the theme for worship. For them to see lovely pictures of nature's glories is one way to help them develop that feeling of thankfulness. Often an arangement of flowers, leaves, or an outdoor setting may achieve the same end.

Did you ever borrow a picture? Do you scan your friends' walls for pictures that might be useful? Most libraries have pictures that can be borrowed. Magazines are full of them if you are awake to your need. Old-book stores are a fruitful place to browse. There are stores that sell old framed pictures at surprisingly low prices. A picture from a magazine, mounted on a cardboard and put into a lovely frame, may be just what you need. Denominational bookstores carry pictures large enough for departmental or large group use. The picture sets, available to you through your own denomination and others, are rich in material not only to aid worship, but for teaching procedures as well.

There are many times when slides shown to the group will create an atmosphere which will blend right into the procedures for worship.

Picture use is one which is too much ignored.

• Look through the pictures you possess and pick out several which you think would help a child in your age group to feel ready for the quietness which may lead to worship; which would help a child enter into the mood for worship; which would bring images to his mind that will aid him to turn to God in thankfulness; which will interpret or introduce some thought that will lead to a desire to worship.

Stories, Verse, and Prose Extracts

There are many collections of stories, poems, and prose extracts to use with children. Your resource here is something like a grocery store! What you need or what must be on your resource shelf or in your mind cannot be just one particular thing. Enough has been said about worship for it to be clear that it is impossible to find all one desires in any one specific book. Exactly what a well-equipped leader will need to guide the children into experiences in which they may worship cannot be confined to one source.

Resource of this kind is everywhere. The trouble is that you cannot rush to the phone and call Mrs. Jones who is your resource in putting on drama, or ask Mr. Wild, who is Bryan's piano teacher, to see that Bryan can play the particular hymn you have decided to use! In this matter you are the one who must become a resource for yourself. You do this by building up, listing, gathering and filing, trying out, learning, being aware of and searching for those stories, poems, and bits of prose. As you do this, you have a store of things which will enable you to go to your "market place" and pick just what is needed so you can make adequate preparation for the spiritual feast which you are to put before the children.

Denominational sources are the best place to start if you are just beginning. You may be inspired to buy some one book which has many lovely things in it. Do not forget that the public library is often a good place to find materials. And why not compare resource with teachers and leaders in other churches of your community?

Screen whatever you clip, copy, or file. Is it true? Is it good? Is it lovely? Will it lead the child's thoughts where you want them to go? Keep the best; discard the rest!

- Do you use stories, poems, and prose selections to lead children to moments of worship? If so, discover for yourself at least two new sources for material. Plan one method to improve the way in which you make this material readily available to yourself.

  Go through what resources you have and pick out the ten most useful stories. Why do you feel each has a direct contribution to make toward worship for the age of child with whom you are working? Go to one story source and find a story that you can see might be used to deepen worship.

  If you are just beginning, choose a poem (it may be from the hymnbook) that will help make your children ready for worship.

  Plan a simple system for keeping the resource materials you discover.

Hymnals

Nursery Songs and Rhythms, by Margaret L. Crain. Judson Press.

Kindergarten Songs and Rhythms. Judson Press.

Home and Church Songs, Bethany Press. (Kindergarten)

Songs for Early Childhood. Westminster Press. (Kindergarten)

*When the Little Child Wants to Sing.** Westminster Press. (Kindergarten)

Songs and Hymns for Primary Children. Westminster Press.

*Hymns for Primary Worship.** Westminster Press.

*Worship and Conduct Songs.** Presbyterian Committee of Publication. (Kindergarten-Primary)

Hymns for Junior Worship. Westminster Press.

Singing Worship, by Edith Lovell Thomas. Abingdon Press. (Junior)

Sing a Tune. Cooperative Recreation Service.

Songs Children Like. Association for Childhood Education International in cooperation with the Division of Christian Education of the National Council of Churches.

The Whole World Singing. Friendship Press.

When Boys and Girls Want to Sing. Warner Press.

Adult and youth hymnals used in your church.

Recordings

Nursery Songs and Rhythms. Judson Press.

Kindergarten Songs and Rhythms. Judson Press.

Home and Church Songs. Bethany Press. (Kindergarten)

Let's Sing Songs for Early Childhood. Westminster Press. (Kindergarten)

---

*Out of print but may be available in many churches and libraries.

Let's Sing Songs and Hymns for Primary Children. Westminster Press.

Let's Sing Hymns for Junior Worship. Westminster Press.

Sing O' Sing. The Graded Press. (Kindergarten)

Gladly Sing. The Graded Press. (Primary)

Growing Days. The Graded Press. (Junior)

Devotional Books for Children

All Through the Year, by Grace W. McGavran. Bethany Press.

As the Day Begins, by Elizabeth McE. Shields. John Knox Press.

Bless This Day, by Elfrida Vipont. Harcourt Brace and Co.

Children's Prayers for Every Day, by Jessie Eleanor Moore. Abingdon Press.

Children's Prayers from Other Lands, by Dorothy Gladys Spicer. Association Press.

Daily Discoveries, by Robbie Trent. Harper & Row.

God, Help Me Understand, by Dorothy Lacroix Hill. Abingdon Press.

God Loves You, by Catherine and Peter Marshall. McGraw-Hill.

Thoughts of God for Boys and Girls, by Welker and Barber. Harper & Row.

Bible Storybooks

Bible Stories, by Mary Alice Jones. Rand McNally.

Bible Stories for Little Children, by Mary Alice Jones. Rand McNally.

Bible Stories for Young Readers, by Edith Patterson. Meyer. Abingdon Press.

Early Old Testament Stories, by Ethel L. Smither. Abingdon Press.

First to Be Called Christians, by Ethel L. Smither. Abingdon Press.

His Name Was Jesus, by Mary Alice Jones. Rand McNally.

Later Old Testament Stories, by Ethel L. Smither. Abingdon Press.

Stories of Jesus, by Ethel L. Smither. Abingdon Press.

The Bible Story for Boys and Girls: Old Testament, by Walter Russell Bowie. Abingdon Press.

The Bible Story for Boys and Girls: New Testament, by Walter Russell Bowie. Abingdon Press.

Background for Parents and Teachers

God, Our Contemporary, by J. B. Phillips. The Macmillan Co.

More Children's Worship in the Church School, by Jeanette Perkins Brown. Harper & Row.

191

Music in the Religious Growth of Children, by Elizabeth McE. Shields. Abingdon Press.

Organizing and Directing Children's Choirs, by Madeline Ingram. Abingdon Press.

The Story of the Bible, by Walter Russell Bowie. Abingdon Press.

The Use of Music in Christian Education, by Vivian Morsch. Westminster Press.

Time for Music—a Guide for Parents, by Landeck. Public Affairs Pamphlet No. 260.